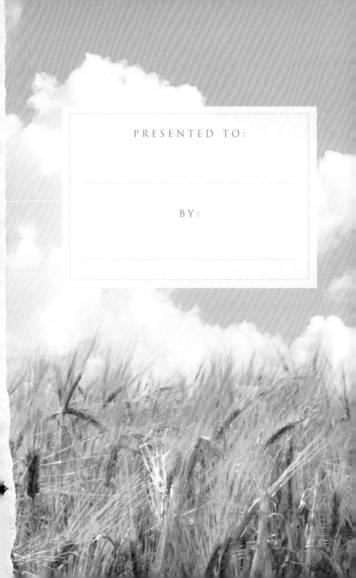

PRESENTED TO:

BY:

The JOY OF MY Heart

ANNE GRAHAM LOTZ

MEDITATING DAILY ON GOD'S WORD

© 2004 Anne Graham Lotz. All rights reserved.

Published by J. Countryman, a division of Thomas Nelson, Inc,
Nashville, Tennessee 37214.

Published in association with the literary agency of
Alive Communications, Inc., 1465 Kelly Johnson Blvd., Suite 320,
Colorado Springs, CO 80920.

Compiled and edited by Terri Gibbs

All Scripture quotations are from the following sources:
The Holy Bible, New International Version. Copyright © 1973
International Bible Society. Used by permission of Zondervan
Bible Publisher.
The King James Version (KJV) of the Bible.
The New King James Version (NKJV®), copyright 1979, 1980,
1982, Thomas Nelson, Inc., Publishers. Used by permission.

Cover designed by Jack Kotowicz, Velocity Design Group.

Interior designed by Robin Black, UDG|DesignWorks,
Sisters, Oregon.

ISBN: 1-4041-0116-0

www.thomasnelson.com
www.jcountryman.com

Printed and bound in Belgium

Your statutes are my heritage forever;
they are the joy of my heart.

PSALM 119:111

Many years ago I began a pilgrimage to know God, and that pilgrimage continues to this day. I don't know Him today as well as I want or should, but I know Him better today than I did twenty-five years ago. I know Him better today than I did one year ago. I am growing in my knowledge of God, and I say without hesitation or qualification that knowing God is my joy and reason for living. He is . . .

the Wind beneath my wings,
the Treasure that I seek,
the Foundation on which I build,
the Song in my heart,
the Object of my desire,
the Breath of my life—
He is my All in all!
And His Word is the joy of my heart!
Please join with me in this life-changing discovery as, day by day, we learn more about our God.

Anne Graham Lotz

January

To know God better
is to love Him more.

THE GOD OF ETERNITY'S BEGINNING

In the beginning God created the heavens and the earth.

GENESIS 1:1, NKJV

⟨⟩ The glorious dawn of God's story begins with the stunning yet profoundly simple statement that in the beginning He created everything (Gen. 1:1)—which means that in the beginning, He was already there. He is eternal.

It is impossible to comprehend eternity. It's been defined as three stages of time: everything before Creation, everything that has taken place or will take place from Creation until the end of the world, and everything that will take place after the end of the world. It stretches back further than the human mind can reach—whether through anthropology, or geology, or archaeology. It stretches ahead further than the human mind can imagine—whether through science fiction, or scientific observation, or telescopes.

God as Creator is eternal and therefore not bound by time. That means He is in your future, and He is in your past, and He surrounds you at present! Would you worship Him now for His eternity?

God's Story

PUTTING HOLES IN THE DARKNESS

*"Let your light so shine before men, that they may see
your good works and glorify your Father in heaven."*

MATTHEW 5:16, NKJV

One night when Robert Louis Stevenson was a small boy, his nanny called him to come to bed. Oblivious to her summons, he was staring at something outside his nursery window. The nanny walked over, stood at his shoulder, and inquired patiently, "Robert, what are you looking at?" The little boy, without taking his eyes away from the window, exclaimed in wonder as he pointed to the lamplighter who was lighting the streetlamps, "Look, Nanny! That man is putting holes in the darkness!"

You and I may not be able to change the world, but surely each of us can put a hole in the darkness! Turn on the Light! Share what Jesus means to you and give God's Word to someone else!

Just Give Me Jesus

HEAVEN IS MORE

Eye has not seen, nor ear heard, nor have entered into the heart of man the things which God has prepared for those who love Him.

1 CORINTHIANS 2:9, NKJV

The Creator Who created all the earthly beauty we have grown to love . . .

the majestic snowcapped peaks of the Alps,

the rushing mountain streams,

the carpets of wildflowers,

the whir of a hummingbird's wings . . .

this is the *same* Creator who has prepared our heavenly home for us! If God could make the heavens and earth as beautiful as we think they are today—which includes thousands of years of wear and tear, corruption and pollution, sin and selfishness—can you imagine what the new Heaven and the new earth will look like? It will be much more glorious than any eyes have seen, any ears have heard, or any minds have ever conceived.

Heaven: My Father's House

JANUARY 4

"GOD SAYS SO" PRAYERS

"If you abide in Me, and My words abide in you, you will ask what you desire, and it shall be done for you."

JOHN 15:7, NKJV

Prayer is a conversation. We speak to God in prayer then listen attentively as He speaks to us through His Word.

Do you think the promise that Jesus gave His disciples was like handing them a Divine Genie in a bottle? And that if they would just rub the bottle with enough faith, the Genie would pop out and grant them their "wishes"? As ludicrous as that is, it actually is the way some people view prayer. And when the Genie doesn't pop out of the bottle, they become offended with God and resent Him for not being at their beck and call.

One major prerequisite to receiving answers to prayer is that our requests line up with God's will. How will we know what God's will is? By abiding consistently in His Word. Instead of basing our prayers on "I hope so," our prayers are based on "God says so." And if we are saturating ourselves in His Word, then His desires will be ours.

My Heart's Cry

MY HOME IS HIS, TOO!

You comprehend my path and my lying down,
and are acquainted with all my ways.

PSALM 139:3

Recently as I prepared my house for a visit by my father, I began to clean and straighten my house. I even bought fresh flowers to place around the rooms. I wanted my home to look as inviting and pleasing to his eyes as I could make it. Then it struck me—if I felt this way about my earthly father's brief visit, how much more care I should give my home every day since my heavenly Father lives here.

I am not a good housekeeper. But motivated by the thought that my house is His home also, I try hard to keep it clean and neat. It is not professionally decorated, but it is as pleasing to the eyes as my time and budget will allow. I want those who walk through my door to know that the Lord God lives here. And I hope the reality of His Presence is evident to all by the beauty of the outward appearance and an inner atmosphere of warmth and love.

God's Story

A LOVE RELATIONSHIP
WITH GOD

God is love, and he who abides in love
abides in God, and God in him.

1 JOHN 4:16, NKJV

The first secret to loving others is to immerse yourself in a love relationship with God the Father, God the Son, and God the Holy Spirit— and abide there.

I will never get over the wonder that God the Father and God the Son do not have

a working kinship

nor a business partnership

nor a brotherly friendship

nor a competing dictatorship

nor a mandatory fellowship

nor an obligatory guardianship

but a love relationship

that has existed since before time and space! And you and I enter into that eternal sphere of unconditional love when we abide in Christ.

My Heart's Cry

LIFE-GIVING POWER

Your word has given me life.

PSALM 119:50, NKJV

Sometimes when we are depressed, we feel lifeless. It's hard to get out of bed in the morning. We seem to have no energy to do even the most routine functions. If you are depressed by the greatness of your problems, read God's Word! That's where you find help. That's where you find joy. Let the rushing waters of the living Word drown out all other sounds and voices. There is life-giving power in the Word of God!

At the most difficult times in my life—the loss of a baby, the forced removal from a church, the execution of a friend, the robbery of our home—God's Word has sustained me. There have been times when I have only been capable of reading a few verses at a time, yet the supernatural life-giving power of the Word of God has not only helped me maintain my emotional and mental balance, it has given me strength to go on, even if only one day at a time.

The Vision of His Glory

A THRILLING ADVENTURE

*"Lord, if it is You, command me
to come to You on the water." So He said, "Come."*
MATTHEW 14:28–29, NKJV

When it comes to experiencing God, I have to choose Him at all cost. I have to be willing to step out of the boat, as Peter did in Matthew 14, risking total failure in the eyes of others, in order to discover firsthand His power enabling me to walk on the water when He bids me, "Come." Again and again, I've been confronted with hard choices when I've had to throw caution to the wind and abandon myself to faith in Him, and Him alone . . .

> when I step into a pulpit,
> when I pick up my pen to write,
> when I hire a new staff person,
> when I commit our ministry to much
more than we have resources to underwrite.

Whenever I choose to step out in faith and trust Him, I'm actually choosing to take Him at His Word, put Him to the test, and *just do it!* The result is the thrilling adventure called the Christian life.

Have you taken the first step?

Why?

WAITING BRINGS BLESSINGS

No one has heard, no ear has perceived,
no eye has seen any God besides you,
who acts on behalf of those who wait for him.

ISAIAH 64:4, NIV

I hate to wait. I hate to wait . . .
for a traffic light to turn green,
for the doctor to see me,
for the telephone to ring,
for investments to produce,
for the copier to warm up,
for seeds to grow,
for the fax to go through,
for answers to prayer . . .
I just hate to wait. Period. Waiting is so hard, especially when I am waiting on the Lord. Sometimes He seems to be *s-o-o-o s-l-o-w*. But waiting is an essential part of spiritual discipline. It can be the ultimate test of our faith.

If we grow impatient with waiting and take matters into our own hands, we will be in trouble. But if we wait on God, we will be blessed.

Just Give Me Jesus

A DAY SET APART

If you call the Sabbath a delight and the LORD's *holy day honorable, . . . then you will find your joy in the* LORD.

ISAIAH 58:13–14, NIV

In the beginning, by His own example, God patterned our week to include not only the discipline of work but also one day out of every seven that would be "set apart," different from the other six days.

For the majority of people today, there is very little difference between the way they keep Sunday and the way they keep Saturday. Sunday has become more of a holiday than a holy day. Sunday was not designed just so we could sleep late, meet friends for brunch, do extra yardwork or housework, attend the latest movie, or watch the playoff game on TV. Sunday should be not only for physical rest and restoration but for spiritual refreshment and expression of our devotion to God.

Has the day that is supposed to be set apart fallen apart? Consider what you can do to keep Sunday special—different from the other six days of the week—and discover "your joy in the Lord."

God's Story

WE ARE GOD'S TREASURE!

"They will be mine," says the LORD *Almighty,*
"in the day when I make up my treasured possession."

MALACHI 3:17, NIV

As we totally yield our lives to the control of God's Spirit within us, He uses:

the responsibilities and relationships and ridicule,

the opportunities and obstacles and obligations,

the pressures and pain and problems,

the success and sickness and solitude. . .

He uses *all things* to work for our ultimate good, which is increasing, progressive, glorious conformity to the image of Jesus Christ. (Rom. 8:28)

We are God's treasure! When God the Father looked throughout the universe for something to give His only Son in reward for what He had accomplished on earth, the Father handpicked you! You are the Father's treasure—His priceless gift of love to the Son!

Heaven: My Father's House

SPEAKING UP FOR JESUS

*"We cannot help speaking about
what we have seen and heard."*

ACTS 4:20, NIV

It has only been a couple of years since our youngest daughter, Rachel-Ruth, gave birth to our first grandchild—a little girl named Ruth Bell Wright. My husband and I are totally enthralled with this little girl. She fills our hearts! We can't help talking about her to anyone who will listen. I'm not afraid to talk about her. I don't plan in advance how I will talk about her. I don't worry about offending someone with my talk about her. I don't go to classes to learn how to talk about her. I don't read books on how to talk about her. I pick up that little girl, feel her snuggle up against me, touch her soft little cheek, and melt! Little Ruth Bell fills my heart! And what fills my heart comes out on my lips!

Why do we seem to make speaking up for Jesus so complicated? If He fills our hearts, He is going to come out on our lips! Like Peter and John, we will not be able to help "speaking about what we have seen and heard" of Him!

My Heart's Cry

THE PROOF OF LOVE

But God demonstrates His own love toward us,
in that while we were still sinners, Christ died for us.

ROMANS 5:8, NKJV

Has someone suggested to you that:
   If God really loved you,
He would heal your disease?
   If God really loved you,
He would never have allowed you to lose your job?
   If God really loved you,
He would bring your spouse back home?
   If God really loved you,
you would be healthy and wealthy and problem free?
Yet God has said that the proof of His love is none
of those things! The proof of His love is that while
we were sinners, passing Jesus by on the road of life,
He sent His only, beloved Son to die for us.

   Would you thank God, not just for saying, "I love
you," in words, but for proving it?

Just Give Me Jesus

JANUARY 14

THE DEVIL'S ALREADY DEFEATED

*The devil, who deceived them, was cast
into the lake of fire and brimstone . . . forever.*
REVELATION 20:10, NKJV

As a girl growing up in western North Carolina, I loved to hike in the mountains. But whenever I set out, my mother's admonition, "Watch out for snakes!" would ring in my ears. Although I can remember killing only one snake myself, I was present several times when snakes were killed by others. Each time I observed a fascinating phenomenon. After the snake was killed, its body invariably continued to twitch until sundown. Even though its head was crushed, rendering it powerless, the dead snake's writhing body was enough to keep me at a distance.

We need to remember that ever since the resurrection of Jesus Christ, Satan has been a defeated foe. His head has been crushed. As we seek to climb higher in our faith, what we are confronted with is merely the twitching of our defeated foe. But sundown is coming! One day even the twitching body of that old Serpent, the devil, will be destroyed.

God's Story

WHEN BAD THINGS HAPPEN

*We know that in all things God works
for the good of those who love him,
who have been called according to his purpose.*

ROMANS 8:28, NIV

Why does God let bad things happen to good people? to innocent people? to children? *to me? Sometimes His ways seem so hard to understand!*

In Romans 8:28, Paul wrote to reassure believers who lived in a city dominated by Nero, a madman with absolute power. He wrote encouragingly, "We know that in all things God works for the good of those who love him, who have been called according to his purpose."

Phrased another way, Paul was reminding the children of God they can be confident that . . .

all things work together for good,
brokenness leads to blessing,
death leads to life,
and suffering leads to glory!

So when bad things happen, just trust Him!

Why?

OUR GOD-GIVEN COUNSELOR

"It is for your good that I am going away.
Unless I go away, the Counselor will not come to you;
but if I go, I will send him to you."

JOHN 16:7, NIV

Following supper the night before He was to be crucified, Jesus unburdened His heart to His disciples. He knew He was going not only to the cross but, after the resurrection, back to His Father in heaven. His disciples would be like orphans. Had He taught them all they needed to know?

The disciples must have begun to sense His heavy burden. Without Jesus, how could they *ever* meet their own needs, much less the needs of the multitude?

Jesus knew their fears. So He began to tell them how they would go on in His absence. He told them they could live, not just somehow, but triumphantly, because "I will not leave you as orphans; I will come to you . . . I will ask the Father, and he will give you *another* Counselor to be with you forever" (John 14:18, 16, NIV, emphasis added). Jesus would remain with them, not physically, but in the invisible person of the Holy Spirit.

Just Give Me Jesus

VALID WORSHIP

God is Spirit, and those who worship Him
must worship in spirit and truth.

JOHN 4:24, NKJV

To worship God means to attribute worth to God through obedience to God, preoccupation with God, and praise of God. The Samaritan woman at the well in Sychar said, in essence, "Oh, well, I worship God." And Jesus corrected her, "You Samaritans worship what you do not know." Why was her worship invalid? Because she was substituting the traditions and rituals of her religion for a personal relationship with God through faith. So Jesus explained, "God is spirit, and his worshipers must worship in spirit and in truth."

To worship God in spirit means to worship Him in deepest sincerity from the heart as one who is indwelled by the Spirit of God. To worship Him in truth means to worship Him honestly, without hypocrisy, through faith in His Word—both the Living Word, which is Jesus, and the written Word, which is the Bible. Is your worship valid?

God's Story

GOD'S ALWAYS AVAILABLE

*Call to Me, and I will answer you, and show you great
and mighty things, which you do not know.*

JEREMIAH 33:3, NKJV

When you approach God through faith in His Son, God is accessible twenty-four hours a day, seven days a week, twelve months a year for the rest of your life!

For the last several years, I have carried a small cellular phone with me whenever I leave the house. Invariably, when I say good-bye to my husband, or speak with my children or staff before I go out of town, I remind them that I will have my phone with me. If I'm needed, all they have to do is call me. Yet how many times have I noticed that I have a voice message waiting on my phone either because it was out of the range of a tower, or I had turned it off while flying, or muted it, or left it in that *other* pocketbook!

Praise God! He is never out of range! He is never turned off or tuned out! His ears are never deaf! He is always available, accessible, and attentive to our call!

My Heart's Cry

GOD OF THE IMPOSSIBLE

"With men this is impossible,
but with God all things are possible."

MATTHEW 19:26, NKJV

What seemingly impossible task has God given you to do? Have you done it, or are you procrastinating? What if Noah had procrastinated and told God he would build the ark but at a time when he felt more capable, when his financial situation was more stable, when his family was more self-sufficient, when it was just more convenient? If he had had the attitude many of us do when God gives us an assignment that is beyond our ability, he would have been totally unprepared for the awesome devastation when it struck.

Instead of procrastination, Noah obeyed without question or hesitation. Noah did everything just as God commanded him (see Gen. 6:22). What impossible task could you accomplish if you would cooperate with God by obeying His Word?

God's Story

GO AND TELL

Many people, because they had heard that he had given this miraculous sign, went out to meet him.

JOHN 12:18, NIV

What has Jesus done for you? What things have your family, friends, neighbors, co-workers, classmates, teammates, employers, employees, professors, doctors, lawyer, counselor, pastor, and anyone else heard about that Jesus has done for you? John testified that, "Many people, because they had heard that he had given this miraculous sign, went out to meet him." Who is seeking to meet Jesus because of what He has done for you?

When have you told someone about how He raised you from spiritual death?

When have you told someone about how He forgave your sin and removed your guilt?

When have you told someone about the disease He healed,

or the prayer He answered,

or the blessing He gave,

or the promise He fulfilled?

Go . . . and tell someone about Jesus!

My Heart's Cry

BASIS FOR HOPE

He who heeds the word wisely will find good,
and whoever trusts in the LORD, happy is he.

PROVERBS 16:20, NKJV

When God told Noah He was "going to bring the floodwaters on the earth to destroy all life under the heavens," He also said He would establish a covenant with Noah and his family to keep them alive along with all the animals who would come to him (Gen. 6:17–18, 20). Noah had God's promise that God would bring him through the Flood to new life on the other side.

Have you been in a situation that has proven to be extremely stressful? Has the pressure been so great that consuming fear and worry have been your constant companions?

When you find yourself drowning in overwhelming circumstances, ask God to give you a promise to cling to—a promise on which you can base your hope. Hope that is based on what you want or what you feel is not a genuine expression of faith. Our hope must be based on God's Word.

God's Story

FOLLOW HIS DIRECTIONS

Blessed are those who keep His testimonies,
who seek Him with the whole heart!

PSALM 119:2, NKJV

God as our Creator has specific directions for our lives. If we live according to His directions, our lives work—we are blessed, and we experience life the way it was meant to be lived. If we ignore or reject His directions, we do so to our own detriment and experience much less than He intended.

All around us are . . .

broken homes,

broken hearts,

broken hopes.

But God never intended us to be broken. He did not just create you and me, plop us down on Planet Earth, and say, "Happy birthday! Now you can guess your way through life." Instead, He has given us directions, which form a pattern that will prevent breakage of our lives and will help to mend the brokenness already present if we follow them.

So . . . open the Creator's manual for life—the Bible—and follow His directions.

God's Story

A GREATER MIRACLE

"Lazarus is dead, and for your sake I am glad I was not there, so that you may believe. But let us go to him."

JOHN 11:14–15, NIV

Jesus was glad Lazarus had *died* without Him?! What does that mean? We know it doesn't mean He enjoyed knowing that Lazarus had died or that He enjoyed thinking about the family's grief and despair.

Jesus was teaching His disciples—and you and me—a life lesson: *There is a greater miracle than physical healing!* It's the miracle of the Resurrection! Be encouraged!

Even if your prayer is not answered
and your loved one is not healed
and your marriage is not reconciled
and your financial problems are
not solved—

there is hope! Jesus was *glad* because He knew God would be glorified to a far greater extent by the death and resurrection of Lazarus than He would have been by Lazarus' healing and recovery from sickness.

Why?

WHAT A SAVIOR!

He came to His own, and His own did not receive
Him. But as many as received Him, to them He gave
the right to become children of God.

JOHN 1:11–12, NKJV

God left His throne at the center of the universe. He set aside His glory, and He humbled Himself as He took on human flesh.

He came to His own—those whom He had created for Himself—but they didn't receive Him.

They contradicted His Word.

They challenged His authority.

They denied His claims.

They questioned His motives.

They mocked His power.

They rejected His Person.

And God in Christ submitted Himself to their slapping, spitting, mocking, taunting, flogging, and stripping, then allowed them to nail Him to a cross where He gave His own life as a sacrifice for their sin. And mine. And yours. His own death satisfied His own judgment for sin, and we are saved. Hallelujah! What a Savior!

God's Story

JANUARY 25

TRUST GOD'S GOODNESS

He will wipe every tear from their eyes.
REVELATION 21:4, NIV

One day God will call us forth from the dead, and we will rise again! Praise God! Praise God! *Praise God!* All of our suffering will be over, and God Himself "'will wipe every tear from their eyes. There will be no more death or mourning or crying or pain, for the old order of things has passed away.' He who was seated on the throne said . . . , 'Write this down, for these words are trustworthy and true'" (Rev. 21:4–5, NIV).

When you don't understand why, just trust Him!
Trust His heart!
Trust His purpose!
Trust His goodness!
Trust His plan to be bigger than yours!
Trust Him because . . . God is enough.

Why?

COME TO HIM

There is no one righteous, not even one.

ROMANS 3:10, NIV

In their pride, the builders of Babel (Gen. 11:4) assumed they could work their way into God's Presence and He would accept them on the basis of what they had done. They were wrong then, and they are still wrong today.

God has said that "All our righteous acts are like filthy rags," (Isa. 64:6, NIV) and "There is no one righteous, not even one," (Rom. 3:10, NIV) and "Without holiness no one will see the Lord" (Heb. 12:14, NIV). So how does one get into heaven? Jesus gave clear instructions, "Not everyone . . . will enter the kingdom of heaven, but only he who does the will of my Father who is in heaven," (Matt. 7:21, NIV) and "I am the way and the truth and the life. No one comes to the Father except through me" (John 14:6, NIV). All religions are man's rebellious, prideful attempt to get around God's stated will and Word. Instead of arguing with Him, just come to Him through Jesus!

God's Story

JANUARY 27

THE GREATEST LIFE

Blessed is the man who trusts in the LORD,
and whose hope is the LORD.

JEREMIAH 17:7, NKJV

Who is Jesus? He lived two thousand years ago, in an obscure town, in an obscure country, during a relatively dark period in human history. Yet He stands unequaled and unparalleled in the stunning impact He has had on history.

As we look back over the past two thousand years, a handful of individuals seem to rise up from our history pages—individuals whose lives impacted the entire human race. Names like Julius Caesar, Martin Luther, Christopher Columbus, Jonas Salk, and Mahatma Gandhi come readily to mind. Yet I would heartily agree with Reynolds Price, who in the introduction to his Time magazine cover story on Jesus, wrote, "It would require much exotic calculation . . . to deny that the single most powerful figure—not merely in these two millenniums but in all human history—has been Jesus of Nazareth." Amen!

Just Give Me Jesus

THE WALK OF FAITH

Enoch walked with God; then he was no more, because God took him away.

GENESIS 5:24, NIV

I wonder what Enoch and God talked about as they walked together each day. Perhaps Enoch commented on the beauty of the sunrise that morning. Or perhaps he told God how grateful he was for the evidence of His faithfulness when he saw the sun come up every morning.

It was never drudgery for Enoch to meet with God. It wasn't something he felt he *had* to do; it was something he *wanted* to do. In the process, he must have grown in an ever more intimate, loving, personal knowledge of Who God is. He gave God his undivided attention, spent more and more time with Him, gained a greater and greater depth of understanding, allowed fewer and fewer interruptions until there were no interruptions at all and his walk of faith became sight!

Enoch's friends looked for him, but he couldn't be found, because he had walked right into the very presence of God!

God's Story

JANUARY 29

DO YOU KNOW HIM?

Your word is settled in heaven.
Your faithfulness endures to all generations.

PSALM 119:89–90, NKJV

The One Who called Abraham out of Ur of the Chaldees, promising to fully bless him if he would follow Him in a life of faith is the same Person Who calls us out of the world and promises to bless us if we follow Him in a life of faith.

The One Who delivered His children from bondage to slavery in Egypt with a titanic display of power is the same Person Who was crucified then rose from the dead to deliver His children today from bondage to sin.

The One Who halted the entire invasion of Canaan by the Israelites while He extended His grace to one Canaanite prostitute is the same Person today Who stops to care for and extend His grace to sinners.

Do you know Him?

Just Give Me Jesus

INVITE THE WORLD!

"In My Father's house are many mansions."

JOHN 14:2, NKJV

Heaven is a big place! "In my Father's house are many mansions"—room enough for anyone and everyone who chooses to be a member of God's family! So please feel free to invite your entire family—including . . .

in-laws and out-laws,

every one of your friends,

all of your neighbors,

the total population of your city,

your state, your nation—

everybody in the whole wide world!

Heaven is a great big place where all are invited to come!

Heaven: My Father's House

A SUITABLE HELPER

Wives, submit to your own husbands. . . .
Husbands, love your wives.
COLOSSIANS 3:18–19, NKJV

The primary reason for woman's creation was not to produce children or provide sexual satisfaction or to keep the home but for the mutual happiness of man and woman. Like the Father of the bride, God Himself brought Eve to Adam.

There is not only an equality but a diversity between men and women. Eve was as different from Adam as Adam was different from Eve. Because of the emotional and physical differences, Eve would supply what Adam lacked, and Adam would supply what Eve lacked. Eve would complete Adam as a "helper suitable for him" (Gen. 2:18, NIV). The same Hebrew word used for "helper" in this instance is used again in Psalm 46:1 when it describes God as being "an ever-present help in trouble." Rather than implying that Eve was somehow less because she was a helper, this term describes her godly characteristic of support for Adam.

God's Story

February

God is greater than we think.

THE SOUND OF HIS VOICE

"My sheep hear My voice,
and I know them, and they follow Me."

JOHN 10:27, NKJV

The Eastern shepherd of Jesus' day raised his sheep primarily in the Judean uplands. The countryside was rocky, hilly, and creased with deep ravines. Patches of grass were sparse. So the shepherd had to establish a personal relationship with each sheep, nurturing its love and trust in order to lead it to where the grass was the greenest, the water was the cleanest, and the nights were the safest. The shepherd always led the sheep. He knew their names, and when he called them, they recognized his voice and, followed him. Their personal relationship with him was based on his voice, which they knew and trusted.

The Bible describes our relationship with Jesus as being similar to the relationship between the Eastern shepherd and his sheep—a relationship based on the sound of His voice. And make no mistake about it, His voice is God's Word, the Holy Bible.

My Heart's Cry

GREATER THAN WE THINK

*His divine power has given to us all things
that pertain to life and godliness, through the knowledge
of Him who called us by glory and virtue.*

2 PETER 1:3, NKJV

God is bigger than we think and greater than
we think. Nothing is beyond His ability, whether it's
> a problem to solve,
>
> a marriage to reconcile,
>
> a memory to heal,
>
> a guilty conscience to cleanse,
>
> a sin to forgive,
>
> a business to save,
>
> a budget to stretch,
>
> another mouth to feed,
>
> or anything else we could name.

All are within His power to "fix." He is more than
able to sustain your marriage and your ministry, your
faith and your finances, your hope and your health.

Just Give Me Jesus

GOD LOVES EVERYONE

Whoever confesses that Jesus is the Son of God,
God abides in him, and he in God.

1 JOHN 4:15, NKJV

God loves each and every person who has ever been born into the human race! God loves:

the Eskimo living in an ice hut,

the Chinese living in a bamboo lodge,

the African living in a mud hut,

the homeless living in a cardboard box,

the Bedouin living in a tent,

the Indian living in a teepee,

the royals living in a palace,

the slum dweller living in a housing project,

God loves the whole world! God loves you! And God loves even me!

Nowhere in the Bible does it say that everyone on Planet Earth is a child of God. But the Bible does say God loves everyone on Planet Earth, and we can call God our Father when we come to Him in a personal relationship through faith in His Son.

God's Story

EVERYTHING WILL BE NEW

Then I saw a new heaven and a new earth,
for the first heaven and the first earth had passed away.
REVELATION 21:1, NIV

Planet earth is, at the very least, thousands of years old. Some think it may be millions or billions of years old. And it is showing signs of age. It is getting frayed and worn out. It is being polluted, gouged, stripped, burned, and poisoned, and much of the damage has been willfully and selfishly inflicted by man. But some of the scars are simply due to the wear and tear of age. It was not created to last forever!

In contrast, our heavenly home is going to be brand-new. Not just restored, but created fresh. What scars of sin or stains of guilt do you bear in your life? . . . in your emotions? in your relationships? in your memories? Like planet earth, do you feel abused and gouged and worn out and burned by other people? One day there will be no more scars. *Everything*—including your heart, mind, emotions, psyche, and memories—will be made new.

Heaven: My Father's House

YOUR FUTURE IS CONFIRMED!

I, John, saw the holy city, . . .
coming down out of heaven from God,
prepared as a bride adorned for her husband.
REVELATION 21:2, NKJV

Regardless of your present
circumstances or crisis,
pressures or pain,
suffering or sorrow,
failures or frustrations,
danger or disease,
memories or misery,
temptations or trials,
problems or persecutions,
burdens or brokenness,
your situation is temporary compared to eternity.
And eternity is going to be spent with Jesus in His
Father's house that has been lovingly prepared just
for you! That's the truth! Your future has been
confirmed!

My Heart's Cry

OPEN THE DOOR TO JESUS

Yet to all who received him, to those who believed in his name, he gave the right to become children of God.
JOHN 1:12, NIV

Most days, my schedule is so packed that although I love my friends, I resist interruptions. Without meaning to be rude, when someone rings the doorbell, I often go to the door, stand inside the house with the screen door still fastened, and talk to the person on the other side. If it is a friend, we can laugh or cry or share common experiences. I don't invite her in because I know if I do, our visit will involve much more time than I can afford to give.

Many people seem to have a "screen door" relationship with Jesus. They talk to Him in prayer, and He talks to them through His Word; they can enjoy His presence, but they never invite Him to come into their lives as Savior and Lord. He's on the outside, looking in. So the apostle John gave you and me motivation to open the door and invite Him to come in: "Yet to all who received him, . . . he gave the right to become children of God." So . . . open the door to Jesus.

Just Give Me Jesus

EASING YOUR BURDEN

*Beloved, let us love one another, for love is of God;
and everyone who loves is born of God and knows God.*

1 JOHN 3:7, NKJV

⟨⟩Most of us increase our pain by dwelling on it or by analyzing it. We throw a pity party and expect others to join us. We spiral downward into depression, withdrawing into self-preoccupation. But the way to overcome is not to focus on ourselves or on the pain, but to focus on the needs of others.

Would you get your eyes off yourself and your problems and your pressures and your pain and look around? Who do you know who is suffering or struggling in some way? What can you do for them? Ask God to bring to your attention those you can care for. Because as you do, you will find joy in easing their burden, and in the process, you will ease your own.

Just Give Me Jesus

THE FOUNDATION FOR FAITH

*"Everyone who hears these words of mine
and puts them into practice is like
a wise man who built his house on the rock."*

MATTHEW 7:24, NIV

On what foundation are you building your life? What feels right? What works? What everyone else is doing?

How stable is your foundation? When an unexpected crisis comes, will your life remain firm and steadfast, or will it all collapse?

The foundation of faith in Jesus Christ is one on which you and I can build our lives with confidence, knowing it will last, not only for our lifetimes but for all eternity as well.

Jesus said, "Everyone who hears these words of mine and puts them into practice is like a wise man who built his house on the rock. The rain came down, the streams rose, and the winds blew and beat against the house; yet it did not fall, because it had its foundation on the rock" (Matt. 7:24–25, NIV). So . . . check your foundation!

God's Story

JOY IN JESUS!

May the God of hope fill you with all
joy and peace in believing, that you may abound
in hope by the power of the Holy Spirit.

ROMANS 15:13, NKJV

Joy is supremely different than happiness. Happiness, which is an American's inalienable right to pursue, seems to depend more on circumstances or things or people or feelings. Joy is independent of everything except our relationship with God. Someone has defined joy as peace dancing! And Jesus, with eyes that must have sparkled in anticipation of the blessing that His beloved friends were going to receive, explained, "I have told you this so that my joy may be in you and that your joy may be complete" (John 15:11, NIV).

One of the hallmarks of those who are immersed in a love relationship with Jesus and His Father, which they express through abiding obedience, is joy! Joy in Jesus! Joy in living our lives for Him! Joy in abiding . . . and obeying! Joy that is complete.

My Heart's Cry

GOD KNOWS

"I know. I know your deeds, your hard work,
your perseverance."
REVELATION 2:2, NIV

How busy are you in Christian service? Are you involved in some type of Christian activity every day of the week? How often are you in church? More than three or four times each week?

Would Jesus say to you, as He did to the Christians at Ephesus: "I know. I know your deeds, your hard work, your perseverance." Did you think Jesus didn't know all that you are doing for Him? Did you think He doesn't see your work behind the scenes, in the kitchen, in the maintenance room, in the nursery, in the parking lot, or in the home—where no one thanks you or encourages you because no one even notices what you do? While others get the attention, the acclaim, the awards, and the affirmation, Jesus says, "I've noticed. I know. Thank you for all you are seeking to do in My Name." Would you accept His encouragement?

The Vision of His Glory

WAIT FOR THE LORD

*Wait for the L*ORD*; be strong and take heart*
*and wait for the L*ORD*.*

PSALM 27:14, NIV

Throughout the Bible, we are given examples of those who waited and were blessed, as well as those who refused to wait and suffered the consequences. For instance:

Abraham had to wait for the birth of Isaac; he grew so impatient, he tried to help God out and had Ishmael instead. His impatience delayed God's blessing for another fourteen years and produced turmoil that exists to this day.

Joshua had to wait seven days as he obediently marched around Jericho before God rewarded his patience and brought the walls down.

David, an anointed king, waited fourteen years in exile before God rewarded his patience by placing him on the throne as the greatest king of Israel. From personal experience he testified, "I am still confident of this: I will see the goodness of the LORD in the land of the living. Wait for the LORD; be strong and take heart and wait for the LORD."

Just Give Me Jesus

WE WERE CREATED TO WORK

"A worker is worthy of his food."
MATTHEW 10:10, NKJV

Jesus Christ knew He had been sent to earth from heaven to save mankind from sin. Yet for thirty years He worked in a carpentry shop in Nazareth. Talk about being overqualified for a job! And although the apostle Paul knew he had been sent from God to evangelize the world, he supported himself and others through tent making.

Very often people refuse to work unless it's in a job that meets their qualifications and goals. All around us are men and women who, when they are laid off, just sit around, send out resumes, and complain that they are out of work. It takes only a glance at the classified ads to know there is plenty of work out there if we are just willing to take on a job we may be very overqualified for or one that doesn't match our lifetime career goals. Any honorable, respectable job is better than no work at all. So . . . stop sitting, keep looking, and start working!

God's Story

FEBRUARY 13

NO MORE TEARS

God will wipe away every tear from their eyes;
there shall be no more death, nor sorrow, nor crying.

REVELATION 21:4, NKJV

One day, God Himself will take your face in
His hands and gently wipe away your tears as He
reassures you there will be no more suffering.

There will be no more . . .

    suicide bombers or fiery infernos,

        broken homes or broken hearts,

            broken lives or broken dreams. . . .

No more cancer or strokes or AIDS. . . .

No more war!

You can look forward with hope, because one
day there will be . . .

    no more separation,

      no more scars,

        no more suffering—

          no more tears at all—

in My Father's House.

Heaven: My Father's House

LOVE WRITTEN IN RED

God so loved the world that He gave
His only begotten Son, that whoever believes in Him
should not perish but have everlasting life.

JOHN 3:16, NKJV

For God so loved you that He gave His Son, His only Son, the Son Whom He loved—He gave heaven's most precious Treasure—He gave everything He had—in order to offer you eternal life.

Do you doubt the love of God? Why? Because of the bad things that He allows to happen to good people? Because of the unfairness and injustice and unkindness and misery and suffering and pain and cruelty of life? Some questions we won't have answers for until we get to heaven. But one thing we can know for sure is that God loves you and me. How do we know that? We know it by just looking at the cross where He proved His love for the world that mocks Him and ignores Him and despises Him and scorns Him and rejects Him.

We look at the cross and see "I love you" written in red—the red of Christ's blood.

Just Give Me Jesus

PARTICIPATING IN A MIRACLE

He took the five loaves and the two fish,
. . . and He blessed and broke them.

LUKE 9:16, NKJV

God never asks us to give Him what we don't have. But He does demand that we give Him all we do have if we want to be a part of what He wishes to do in the lives of those around us!

Remember the servants at the wedding in Cana? They had the thrill of knowing firsthand that water went into the pitcher, but wine came out! They had the unparalleled experience of participating in a miracle! Could you be in danger of missing the thrilling blessing of participating with God in a miracle because, for whatever reason, you won't give Him all that you have? The disciples did not know it at the time, but they were on the verge of participating in a miracle because they gave Jesus everything they had found to feed the crowd: five barley loaves and two small fish! As a result, the entire multitude was fed—and blessed!

Just Give Me Jesus

PARADISE REGAINED!

"The man . . . must not . . . take also from
the tree of life and eat, and live forever." So the
LORD God banished him from the Garden of Eden.

GENESIS 3:22–23, NIV

Adam and Eve were driven from their garden home, driven from security and safety, and separated from God! The loneliness and desperate agony of loss must have been overwhelming. As they looked back, they could see at the entrance to what had been their home a powerful angel standing guard with a sword swirling like a mad dervish, preventing any thought of return. The finality of their separation from all they had been created for must have been devastating.

Since there was only one entrance into the Garden and it was guarded carefully and constantly, it was not just hard to get back into God's presence— it was impossible! Neither Adam nor Eve, nor you nor I, nor anyone ever born into the human race could ever get back into God's Presence. Heaven can never be gained through human effort. Paradise was lost! But, praise God! Heaven's door is opened and paradise regained at the cross.

God's Story

FEBRUARY 17

ON WINGS OF FAITH

Suddenly there came a sound from heaven,
as of a rushing mighty wind, . . . and they were
all filled with the Holy Spirit.

ACTS 2:2-4, NKJV

I understand that a turkey and an eagle react differently to the threat of a storm. A turkey reacts by running under the barn, hoping the storm won't come near. On the other hand, an eagle leaves the security of its nest and spreads its wings to ride the air currents of the approaching storm, knowing they will carry it higher in the sky than it could soar on its own. Based on your reaction to the storms of life, which are you? A turkey or an eagle?

It's natural for me to be a turkey in my emotions, but I have chosen to be an eagle in my spirit. And as I have spread my wings of faith to embrace the "Wind," placing my trust in Jesus and Jesus alone, I have experienced quiet, "everyday" miracles:

His joy has balanced my pain.

His power has lifted my burden.

His peace has calmed my worries.

So . . . would you spread your wings of faith and soar?!

Why?

THE SOLUTION TO SIN

But now in Christ Jesus you who once were far away
have been brought near through the blood of Christ.
EPHESIANS 2:13, NIV

God is righteous and just. But God is also loving and merciful. He cannot be less than Himself. Satan, in his temptation of Adam and Eve and in his plan to defeat the purpose of God, failed to take into account the very character of God. He failed to realize one very important thing—how much God loved the man and woman He had created and the depths to which His grace would go in order to bring them back to Himself. It never entered Satan's wicked, self-centered imagination that God would commit the fullness of His eternal, divine nature to bring man back into a right relationship with Himself. It never occurred to Satan, who ever seeks his own preeminence, that the Creator of the universe would lay down His own life in atonement for man's sin. But that's exactly what happened. The solution to the problem of sinfulness is the cross of Jesus Christ.

God's Story

FILLED WITH THE SPIRIT

Be filled with the Spirit.
EPHESIANS 5:18, NIV

God has clearly commanded you and me to "be filled with the Spirit." But an unconfessed sin or resistance to His authority will block the "flow" of His life within us. If we do not deal with it, our spiritual lives become stagnant and we lose our attractiveness and usefulness to God. And we have nothing refreshing about us that would draw other people to Christ.

What is hindering you from being filled with the Holy Spirit? To be filled with the Holy Spirit is to be under His moment-by-moment control. He has not been given to you so that you can keep Him confined to a particular area in your life. Let Him loose! He is Lord! The amount of power you experience to live a victorious, triumphant Christian life is directly proportional to the freedom you give the Spirit to be Lord of your life! *Just Give Me Jesus*

WALKING WITH GOD

Cause me to know the way in which I should walk,
for I lift up my soul to You.

PSALM 143:8, NKJV

Every morning that I'm home, weather permitting, I walk with two friends for two and a half miles. We abide by two basic rules when we walk: we walk at the same pace and we walk in the same direction. The same two rules apply when walking with God.

To walk at the same pace means that we are living our lives in step-by-step obedience to His Word. To walk in the same direction means that we surrender the direction of our lives to Him. The only way we can know His pace and direction is to prayerfully read His Word.

What adjustments do you need to make so you can walk with God? Adjustments in your daily and weekly schedule? Adjustments in your attitude and ambition? Make sure you are not too busy for daily prayer and Bible reading or you will get out of step and lose your sense of direction.

God's Story

CALL HIM "DADDY"

You received the Spirit of sonship.
And by him we cry, "Abba," Father.
ROMANS 8:15, NIV

What makes you and me think we can do without a personal prayer life? It's through prayer that we come into a personal, intimate relationship with our heavenly Father.

Do you long to have a closer relationship with God, but you don't feel worthy? Are you convinced you are a nobody and therefore would never be accepted, much less welcomed, into His presence?

Praise God! Our entrance into His presence is not based on our own worthiness but on the worthiness of Jesus Christ! When we enter God's presence in Jesus' name, we are as accepted by God as Jesus is, because God counts us as His own dear children!

Jesus invites you and me, in His name, to come into His Father's presence through prayer, crawl up into His lap by faith, put our head on His shoulder of strength, feel His loving arms of protection around us, call Him "Abba" Daddy, and pour out our hearts to Him.

My Heart's Cry

CREATED TO KNOW GOD

*"Now this is eternal life: that they may know you, the
only true God, and Jesus Christ, whom you have sent."*

JOHN 17:3, NIV

Man was created
to walk and talk with God,
to love and obey God,
to listen to and learn from God,
to glorify and enjoy God forever!
Jesus defined our meaning for existence when
He prayed, "Now this is eternal life: that they may
know you, the only true God, and Jesus Christ,
whom you have sent." Knowing God in a personal
and permanent relationship is the ultimate human
experience. Knowing God is the meaning of human
life. It is the reason for our existence. It was the
completion of all the changes God made in the
environment in the beginning. And it is the
completion of all the changes God is making in your
life at the present.

Get to know Him and discover the real meaning
of life.

God's Story

PRAISE DEFEATS THE ENEMY

I will declare Your name to My brethren;
in the midst of the assembly I will praise You.
PSALM 22:22, NKJV

One way to drive Satan to distraction, and to overcome him, is through praise of Jesus. Regardless of whether the enemy is a visible foe in front of us like the Scribes and Pharisees or an invisible foe outside of us like the devil himself or an invisible foe inside of us like depression, praise drives the enemy away. In the very prophecy that describes Jesus' inmost thoughts and feelings as He hung on the cross, tortured, bleeding, and dying, the psalmist declared, "But You are holy, enthroned in the praises . . ." of Your people (Ps. 22:3, NKJV). In other words, He is enthroned—He rules in power, authority, and supremacy—through our praise.

In some supernatural way, praise ushers the authority of God into any given situation. One practical way to maintain your praise is, every time you pray, to begin your prayer with praise. First praise Him for Who He is. Then praise Him for something He has done for you. Start now!

My Heart's Cry

GOD IS FAITHFUL!

His compassions fail not. They are new every morning;
great is Your faithfulness.

LAMENTATIONS 3:22–23, NKJV

Three hundred and seventy-one days after the Flood began, "God said to Noah, 'Come out of the ark, you and your wife and your sons and their wives'" (Gen. 8:15, NIV). We can almost hear the "Hallelujah Chorus" playing in the background! What a day of rejoicing that must have been! God had been faithful to see him through!

God has not changed. If He was faithful to watch over Noah and all those within the ark, bringing them safely through the storm, He will do the same for you. Just as He was faithful to preserve Joseph through thirteen years of slavery in Potiphar's house and Pharaoh's prison, just as He was faithful to preserve the little baby Moses floating on the Nile . . . *God will be faithful to you.* Why? Because God is faithful! He cannot be less than Himself! Keep your focus on God's faithfulness and on God's greatness!

God's Story

NAMING YOUR SIN

*That you may know that the Son of Man
has power on earth to forgive sins.*

MATTHEW 9:6, NKJV

God promises, "If we confess our sins, he is faithful and just and will forgive us our sins" (1 John 1:9, NIV). That word *confess* means to call sin by the same names that God does, to agree with God about your sin.

You and I often play games with the names we call sin to make it seem less like sin. For example, we call the sin of unbelief, worry. We call the sin of lying, exaggeration. We call the sin of fornication, safe sex.

As long as we switch the labels on sin to make it seem less serious, we're being dishonest with ourselves and with God, and we remain unforgiven. *But,* if we say the same thing about our sin that God says—if we say, "God, it's lying. It's jealousy. It's lust. It's revenge. It's hate. It's adultery. It's unforgiveness" —*God will forgive us!*

So start naming your sin for what it is in God's eyes.

Just Give Me Jesus

DON'T TOLERATE TEMPTATION!

Submit to God. Resist the devil
and he will flee from you.
JAMES 4:7. NKJV

Temptation, whether in the form of a serving of birthday cake when you're on a diet or the bed of your neighbor's spouse, intensifies through toleration. The toleration leads to a preoccupation of thoughts, and it's not long before we reach out to touch it. At that point, there is almost no turning back.

What temptation have you tolerated, thought about, touched, and toyed with? "It's just one more glass of wine." "It's just a little harmless flirtation." "It's just a magazine at the checkout counter." "It's just one date." Watch out! If you tolerate it, think about it, and toy with it, you are just a step away from actually doing it.

So . . . instead of tolerating sin, turn from it NOW!

God's Story

PRECIOUS IN GOD'S SIGHT

When you pass through the waters, I will be with you.
ISAIAH 43:2, NIV

Have your thoughts been similar to these?
> *God, where have You been?*
> *Why did You let this happen?*
> *I just don't understand.*

Are you overlooking the fact that Jesus has drawn near to you?

Are you blinded to His presence by your own tears?

Are you deafened to His gentle voice by your own accusations?

While God doesn't always protect those He loves from suffering or answer our prayers the way we ask Him to, He does promise in His Word that He will be present with us in the midst of our suffering and pain. He said, "Fear not. . . . When you pass through the waters, I will be with you; and when you pass through the rivers, they will not sweep over you. . . . For I am the LORD, your God . . . your Savior; . . . you are precious and honored in my sight, and . . . I love you" (Isa. 43:1–4, NIV).

Why?

KEEP YOUR FOCUS

The word of the LORD is proven;
He is a shield to all who trust in Him.

PSALM 18:30

God, as the Judge of all the earth, determined the wickedness of Cain's civilization could no longer be tolerated, and He sent the Flood to wash it away. God, Who judged the world, is the same God Who saved the world from His own judgment by providing the ark as a means of escape. Praise God! That's His goodness!

Like pouring oil on troubled waters, our knowledge of Who God is calms our fears. So . . . keep your faith, and keep your focus!

God is faithful
    and gracious
        and good
            and loving
                and patient
                    and holy
                        and righteous
                          and merciful.

God's Story

March

❧

We are totally helpless without God.

GRINDING OFF THE SHARP EDGES

"My command is this: Love each other
as I have loved you."
JOHN 15:12, NIV

In the Old Testament, the meal offering consisted of fine flour that was ground to powder by being placed in a round hole, where it was grated by a square pestle. The flour was then mixed with oil, which represented the Holy Spirit. The oil and flour, thoroughly mixed together and offered to God, was a picture of a totally consecrated life.

Sometimes God puts us with someone whom He uses to grate us. Perhaps you are very quiet, and God has put you on a committee with someone who talks nonstop. Or worse, perhaps you are a nonstop talker and you are on a committee with another nonstop talker! Instead of avoiding those with whom we are incompatible or just tolerating them, Jesus commands you and me to love them. And as we obey His command, He will use that person to grind off our sharp, impatient, un-Christlike edges.

My Heart's Cry

MARCH 2

GOD THE LIVING WORD

In the beginning was the Word,
and the Word was with God, and the Word was God.
JOHN 1:1, NIV

John's Gospel begins with the astounding statement that "In the beginning was the Word." The Greek translation for "word" is *logos*, which means the outward expression of all that God is. Plato once said that he hoped one day there would come a "logos" from God that would make everything clear. John said He has come! "And the Word was with God . . ." as another separate, supreme Being. "And the Word was God." Although the Word is another separate Person from God the Father, He is no less in power, position, or personality. Because He is God the Creator! "Through him all things were made. . . . We have seen his glory, the glory of the One and Only Son who came from the Father, full of grace and truth"(John 1:14, NIV).

The "One and Only Son who came from the Father" is the *logos* of God through Whom God created everything, and His name is JESUS!

God's Story

NO NIGHT THERE

The city does not need the sun or the moon
to shine on it, for the glory of God gives it light,
and the Lamb is its lamp.

REVELATION 21:23, NIV

Our heavenly home will glow and radiate with light from within—the light of God Himself and the glorious radiance of His presence.

I have been in some of the great cities of the world at night. I have looked out after sunset from Victoria Peak in Hong Kong during the Chinese New Year, and I have seen the lights transform the hills surrounding the harbor into a virtual fairyland. I have seen the lights of Capetown, South Africa, wrapped around Table Mountain at night forming a vast, jewel-studded skirt.

But even in those great cities with their millions of lights, there are still pockets of darkness. In our heavenly home, there will be no darkness at all.

Heaven: My Father's House

YOU'RE WELCOME

"In my Father's house are many rooms;
if it were not so, I would have told you.
I am going there to prepare a place for you."

JOHN 14:2, NIV

How often I have dashed home from church to get things ready for guests I have invited to lunch! I want to get the ice in the glasses, take the roast out of the oven while I pop the rolls in, make the gravy, steam the broccoli, and generally get things organized so that when my guests walk through the door everything is prepared for their enjoyment. I want them to know by the delicious aromas coming from the kitchen, and the elegant setting of the table, and the sideboard laden with dishes brimming with steaming food that they are expected and they are welcome.

In John 14:2, Jesus was telling His disciples that He was going to dash Home to get things ready for them so when they walked through the door they would know they were expected, they were welcome, and His Home was theirs to enjoy!

My Heart's Cry

BELIEVE IN HIS NAME

There is no other name under heaven
given among men by which we must be saved.

ACTS 4:12, NKJV

Although God is the Creator of us all, nowhere does the Bible say we are all His children. On the contrary, there are two conditions you and I must meet before we can be called God's children. One is that we must receive Jesus, or open the door of our hearts and invite Him to come in. The other is that we must believe in His Name.

Believing in His Name means we must be willing to commit our lives to all that He is as represented by His Name. And His Name is *Lord Jesus Christ.*

The qualification for being a child of God by believing on His Name means much more than just head knowledge. It is not just giving intellectual assent to the fact that the name Lord Jesus Christ is the label attached to the Person. It means to rest in Jesus, to put all of our trust on Him alone for forgiveness and salvation.

Just Give Me Jesus

FOLLOW THE LIGHT

Your word is a lamp to my feet and a light for my path.

PSALM 119:105, NIV

In what area of your life do you need illumination? Discouragement about the future and the direction we have chosen, depression over the lack of fulfillment in our lives, or disillusionment by our previous attempts to find meaning for life through organized religions can all plunge us into the darkness. Do you ever wonder,

"What is the meaning to my life?"

"Why is genuine happiness so elusive?"

"Why do I feel guilty?"

"Why do I feel afraid?"

"Is there a God?"

"Is there life after death?"

God's written Word and the answers we find there turn our darkness into light. God's Word "is a lamp to my feet and a light for my path."

So . . . follow the light!

God's Story

GOD'S LOVE

God has poured out his love into our hearts
by the Holy Spirit, whom he has given us.

ROMANS 5:5, NIV

Did you know that you are God's special loved one? Why would He love you so? Maybe it's because when you abide in Christ you are so saturated in Jesus that when God looks at you, He sees His own precious Son and envelops you in His love for Jesus' sake!

As you and I develop and grow in this love relationship with God, abiding with Him through meaningful prayer and Bible reading, getting to know Him on a deeper level as we live out what we say we believe, He fills us with Himself. And "God is love" (1 John 4:16, NKJV). As you and I are filled with God, we will be filled with His love, not only for Himself, but for others—which includes our spouses or the incompatible people with whom we are struggling. God has promised to pour out "his love into our hearts by the Holy Spirit, whom he has given us."

My Heart's Cry

TWO TOGETHER FOREVER

*A man will leave his father and mother and
be united to his wife, and they will become one flesh.*

GENESIS 2:24, NIV

Some people may consider the intimate side of marriage as somehow being "unspiritual." But if you stop to think about it, the first person who ever had a sexual thought was God. Love expressed in marriage in a mutually respectful sexual relationship is God's idea, and it is pure, holy, and pleasing to Him.

Dr. Ed Wheat, a prominent marriage counselor, has pointed out that if the physical side of marriage deteriorates, every other aspect of marriage will soon be affected (*Love Life*). When God commanded Adam and Eve to "be fruitful and increase in number" (Gen. 1:28, NIV), He seemed to be saying, "Make sex a priority in your marriage," not only for the procreation of the race but also in order to maintain the intimate physical unity with each other that we were created for.

God's Story

OPEN YOUR EYES

"He will bring glory to me by taking from what is mine and making it known to you."

JOHN 16:14, NIV

Without the Holy Spirit to clarify the truth to our minds and confirm Who Jesus is in our hearts, we would "see" Jesus as just . . .

a man,

or a holy man,

or a prophet,

or a symbolic figure!

But the Holy Spirit opens our eyes to see and our minds to know and our hearts to receive that Jesus is more than just a man . . . or a prophet . . . or a teacher . . . or a revolutionary . . . or an icon . . . or a symbol. Jesus is . . .

the Messiah of Israel,

the Son of God,

the Savior of the world,

the reigning King . . .

God Himself in the flesh!

My Heart's Cry

HUMBLE SUBMISSION

*Jesus came with them to . . . Gethsemane, and said
to the disciples, "Sit here while I go and pray over there."*

MATTHEW 26:36, NKJV

The betrayal and arrest of Jesus was preceded by an extended time of prayer in the Garden of Gethsemane. When He stepped out of the garden to present Himself to His enemies, Jesus had been alone, praying and agonizing for hours, wrestling with the will of His Father for His life, sweating what seemed to be great drops of blood in His effort.

His humble submission to His Father's will must have given Him a mantle of power that cloaked Him for the nine-hour journey that would take Him through six different trials, the inhumane cruelty of physical torture, the ultimate rejection of those He loved, and the climax of His own crucifixion and death on a Roman cross.

How is it that you and I think we can make it through the grueling journey of life without that same humble submission to the Father?

Just Give Me Jesus

LAY YOUR GRIEVANCES DOWN

Do not be overcome by evil, but overcome evil with good.

ROMANS 12:21, NIV

I was a state witness to the execution of Velma Barfield, the first woman to be executed in the United States in more than twenty-two years. I had developed a friendship with her about six months prior to her execution and had grown to love her as a sister in Christ. Following the execution, a newspaper reporter asked, "Anne, how are you going to get back at the state? Aren't you bitter?"

I knew I could let the grief over my friend's death become a grievance that would turn into bitterness. But by God's grace, I chose to take my reaction to the cross of Christ. In prayer, I had to leave the anger and bitterness with the One Who said, "It is mine to avenge; I will repay" (Rom. 12:19, NIV).

I laid my grievances at the nail-pierced feet of One Who understands firsthand what it feels like to be deeply wounded by the sin of other people. Would you do the same?

God's Story

THE PAIN OF BETRAYAL

*Jesus said to him, "Judas, are you
betraying the Son of Man with a kiss?"*

LUKE 22:48, NKJV

Judas was one of Jesus' very closest friends. He had been handpicked to be a disciple. He had been given the special responsibility of being treasurer for the entire band of disciples—a responsibility he had enjoyed as it gave him access to personal petty cash as well as prestige in the eyes of others. Yet it was this disciple who betrayed his Lord and Friend with a kiss! And although Jesus clearly knew the betrayal was coming, it was still a knifelike stab to His heart.

Have you ever been betrayed . . .

by a spouse who has taken a secret lover?

by a sibling who has stolen your inheritance?

by a coworker who has taken the credit for a job you did?

If you have experienced betrayal, then you understand something of the stabbing pain Judas inflicted at the very outset of Jesus' uphill struggle to the cross and you would resolve never to betray another.

Just Give Me Jesus

THE JOY OF MY HEART   85

HELPLESS WITHOUT HIM

*"I do not seek My own will
but the will of the Father who sent Me."*

JOHN 5:30, NKJV

Have you wondered, in agony, why God is doing what He's doing? Why He has delayed answering your prayer? Have you reacted to the delay by trying to help Him out and speed things up? Have you turned to . . . a doctor, a lawyer, a counselor, a friend, pop psychology, a neighbor's sympathetic ear, or a popular TV talk show? Have you resorted to threats or bargaining or manipulation until you're totally exhausted? Have you come to the absolute end of your rope?

One reason God may be delaying His answer to your prayer and postponing His intervention in your situation is to bring you to the end of your own resources. Sometimes God waits in order to allow us time to exhaust every other avenue of help until we finally realize without any doubt or reservation that we are totally helpless without Him.

Why?

THE HEARTBEAT OF JESUS

"Father, I want those you have given me to
. . . see . . . the glory you have given me because you
loved me before the creation of the world."
JOHN 17:24, NIV

Before the foundation of the world was laid, God, in His divine sovereignty, planned to send His own Son to the cross to be our Savior. Before the beginning of time and space and human history, He took counsel with Himself and decided to bring us into existence, knowing full well that we would rebel against Him and become separated from Him by our sin. So He made preparations for our redemption—preparations that were finished once and for all time at the cross.

The heartbeat of Jesus was to finish His Father's plan and, in so doing, bring glory to God. In other words, through His own death on the cross, Jesus would reveal the love of God in such a way that people throughout the ages would praise Him and love Him and lay down their lives before Him. So He embraced the cross and all that it meant.

My Heart's Cry

BOUND IN GOD'S WILL

They laid their hands on Him and took Him.

MARK 14:46, NKJV

The soldiers and officials who had come to the Garden of Gethsemane to arrest Jesus seized Him roughly, punching and manhandling Him as they bound Him. *They bound the hands* of the Son of God! *The hands of the Creator!* Hands that had lifted in authority and calmed the storm at sea. Hands that had gathered little children on His knee.

Have you ever felt bound . . .

in a marriage where the love has run out?

in a home with small children?

in a body wracked with pain?

Are you struggling with your bindings? Do you find that the more you fight against them, the more pain you inflict on yourself, so that you are miserable in your confinement? Sometimes binding is in the will of God. Jesus was in the center of His Father's will, yet He was bound. He did not resist the tight cords or complain about His confinement. He simply submitted, not to the soldiers, but to His Father's will. Would you do the same?

Just Give Me Jesus

HUNGRY FOR GOD

*If anyone is in Christ, he is a new creation, old things
have passed away; behold all things have become new.*

2 CORINTHIANS 5:17, NKJV

The changes brought about by God's Word
in your life and mine are not primarily for the
purpose of making us good or successful or happy
or wealthy or prosperous or problem free. The
primary purpose of these changes is that we might
know God fully and intimately so we can reflect
Him in all we are and say and do, bringing glory to
the One Who created us.

Is your life complete? Do you feel you are
waiting for something, but you don't know what?
Do you have an aching loneliness, a hunger pain of
the spirit, a yearning deep inside yourself for
something? For Someone? Then get in touch with
your Creator. You are hungry for God. You were
created with a capacity to know Him in a personal,
permanent, love relationship. That capacity is
empty until you establish the relationship with Him
for which you were created.

God's Story

BETRAYAL

"Why do you call me 'Lord, Lord,'
and not do the things which I say?"

LUKE 6:46, NKJV

———

Within moments of betraying Jesus, Judas hated himself for what he had done. Jesus' third religious trial was interrupted briefly by a commotion at the doorway as Judas burst onto the scene. With a face that was surely contorted by the wretchedness of conviction, he flung thirty pieces of silver across the temple floor. As the room suddenly grew silent, the clattering coins must have reverberated in the stillness as they skidded across the marble surface. Thirty pieces of silver! The price of a wounded slave! (see Ex. 21:32) Judas sold his Lord for *the price of something that was good for nothing!*

You and I betray Jesus when we call ourselves Christians yet give our hearts to money, or material things, or selfish pursuits, or anyone or anything other than Him. Would you confess and repent of your sin of betrayal and commit to living a life of love and loyalty to Jesus?

Just Give Me Jesus

LISTENING CAREFULLY

I rejoice at Your word as one
who finds great treasure. . . . I love Your law.
PSALM 119:162–163, NKJV

When have you totally misunderstood God's Word?

When He said, "Love one another,"
did you think He meant to tolerate sin? (1 John 4:7)

When He said, "in all things God works for the good," did you think that every story has a happy ending? (Rom. 8:28)

Listening carefully to what God says is important, because if we misunderstand what He is saying, we set ourselves up for disappointment, discouragement, and disillusionment.

So . . . would you be quiet and listen with your eyes on the pages of your Bible? Listen for His still, small voice to whisper to your heart through His Word.

Why?

ACCOUNTABLE BEFORE GOD

*"To whom much is given, from him much will
be required; and to whom much has been committed,
of him they will ask the more."*

LUKE 12:48, NKJV

When Annas the high priest questioned Jesus (John 18:19), Jesus answered directly, "I have spoken openly to the world . . . I always taught in synagogues or at the temple, where all the Jews come together. I said nothing in secret. Why question me? Ask those who heard me. Surely they know what I said" (John 18:20–21, NIV).

Jesus confronted Annas with the awesome principle that God holds people accountable, not just for what they have heard or know, but for what they have had *opportunity* to hear and know. And in America, with churches on every corner, with religious radio broadcasts, with Christian television programming, *America has enormous accountability before God!*

It doesn't matter if you have ever tuned in to or listened to any of the above. You and I have had the opportunity to do so, and for that we will be held accountable by God.

Just Give Me Jesus

UNITED IN PRAISE

I will greatly rejoice in the LORD,
my soul shall be joyful in my God.

ISAIAH 61:10, NKJV

Who is praising Jesus because you are? If your praise—and mine—is interrupted by . . .

our circumstances or our complaints,

our selfishness or our suffering,

our desires or our depression,

our indifference or our insistence,

or by anything at all . . .

the light will grow dim in our lives as we sink into the mire of self, and instead of causing others to praise Him, we will drag them down into the darkness with us.

So would you praise Him? And keep on praising Him! Praise Him for _____. You fill in the blank with an attribute of Christ.

My Heart's Cry

THE LOOK OF JESUS

While [Peter] was still speaking, the rooster crowed.
And the Lord turned and looked at Peter.

LUKE 22:60-62, NKJV

The night Jesus was betrayed, a man stepped up to Peter in the courtyard of the temple compound and challenged him: "Didn't I see you with [Jesus] in the olive grove?" (John 18:26, NIV). All the tension and anger of the past hours exploded in Peter and tumbled out in a stream of curses as he insisted, "I don't know the man!" Yet as he spoke, he heard the unmistakable sound of a rooster crowing in the distance. At that very moment, a commotion in the breezeway got everyone's attention. With the denial still burning his lips, Peter looked into the eyes of Jesus! Shaken to the core of his being, Peter went out into the night, where he "wept bitterly."

Three days later, Peter knew his sin had been forgiven when he met the risen Christ. Is your heart burning with shame and guilt? Don't shed tears, shed your pride and come to Jesus for cleansing and restoration.

Just Give Me Jesus

THE SIGN OF THE CROSS

"This is My blood of the new covenant,
which is shed for many for the remission of sins."
MATTHEW 26:28, NKJV

God knew that after our salvation experience, as we sought to live a new life, we would sin again. And because of the continuing struggle with sin and failure in our lives, we would be tempted to doubt our salvation. So God gave us a sign of the new covenant. Jesus said it was the sign of His broken body and His poured-out blood. It was the sign of the cross.

Have you become so overwhelmed with your own weakness and failure and sin and inability to live a life that is pleasing to God that you have begun to doubt your salvation? Then look up! Take a good, long look at the cross and remember that *God remembers*. He loves you, He has forgiven you, He is eternally committed to you, and you are saved! Forever! Praise God! His covenant is unconditional!

God's Story

THE ANTIDOTE TO FEAR

"Trust in God; trust also in me."

JOHN 14:1, NIV

Jesus commanded His disciples to "trust in God; trust also in me." The antidote to fear is *faith*.

When I toss and turn in the middle of the night, worried and fearful over something that is impending in my life or the life of someone I love, I am comforted and calmed as I meditate on Who God is. It helps me plant my faith in Someone Who is bigger than my fears. I just fall back on Who God is and rest in Him. He cannot be less than Himself! And my God is God!

Next time you feel afraid, make up a list—not of your fears but of the characteristics of God. Find a Scripture verse or passage to substantiate each one as you reconsider your situation in light of Who God is. Then, if you feel it would be helpful to list your fears, make sure beside each one you write down the attribute of God that applies. The secret to peace lies in your focus.

My Heart's Cry

THANK HIM NOW

He was pierced for our transgressions,
he was crushed for our iniquities.
ISAIAH 53:5, NIV

Perhaps thinking to satisfy the crowd's thirst for blood without actually going so far as to execute Jesus, Pilate had Him flogged. History records that flogging victims either passed into unconsciousness, went insane, or died. The miracle is not that Jesus survived the whipping, but that *He submitted to it!* How easy it would have been for Him to defy them and, without cursing but in righteous judgment, send them all to hell!

Why? *Why* would God allow His Son to endure such physical torture? The answer had been given years earlier, when Isaiah solemnly prophesied, "Surely he took up our infirmities and carried our sorrows. . . . He was pierced for our transgressions, he was crushed for our iniquities; the punishment that brought us peace was upon him, and by his wounds we are healed" (Isa. 53:4–5, NIV).

Just Give Me Jesus

GOD LIFTS THE PRESSURE

The LORD will give strength to His people;
the LORD will bless His people with peace.

PSALM 29:11, NKJV

Do you feel overwhelmed and smothered by pressure? Are you desperate for "breathing room"? Do you try to escape the stress through . . .

an extended vacation,

therapeutic counseling,

alcohol,

drugs,

entertainment, or

a romantic liaison . . .

only to find when you stop to assess your condition you are no better than you were before, because the pressure is from within?

Only God has the power to lift the pressure from within you. Your circumstances may remain the same, but He has the power to give you breathing room. He can give your spirit peace and rest, even as He gives your life a new dimension. Just ask Him.

God's Story

SET FREE!

*You have been set free from sin
and have become slaves to righteousness.*

ROMANS 6:18, NIV

With blood flowing from His wounds and streaming down His face from the thorns in His brow, Jesus stood before Pilate. As part of the Passover celebration, it was Pilate's custom to release any prisoner the crowd chose. It just so happened that "at that time they had a notorious prisoner, called Barabbas. So . . . Pilate asked them, 'Which one do you want me to release to you: Barabbas, or Jesus Who is called Christ?'" (Matt. 27:16–17, NIV).

The rulers shouted back, "No, not him! Give us Barabbas!" (John 18:40, NIV). *Barabbas!* Barabbas was a thief and a murderer and a rabble-rouser! The religious leaders of Israel were demanding that Barabbas be set free and Jesus be crucified. And so Barabbas became the first person to be set free by the death of Jesus.

Jesus died, not just in the place of Barabbas, but in your place and mine. Because He died, I am free! Free from my sin and its penalty. *Just Give Me Jesus*

MARCH 27

THE SILENCE OF GOD

He who trusts in the LORD,
mercy shall surround him.

PSALM 32:10, NKJV

Is God silent in your life? What prayers has He not answered for you?

At a time of unanswered prayer in my life years ago, my mother taught me the verse to a hymn that I still quote when I am totally baffled by events that seem to career out of the orbit of what I have asked:

> Trust Him when dark doubts assail thee,
> Trust Him when thy strength is small,
> Trust Him when to simply trust Him,
> Seems the hardest thing of all.

Is your focus on your immediate need blinding you to a greater purpose that God is working out? Would you choose to be patient and simply trust Him? Sometimes God does not answer our immediate prayer because He has something greater in store for us.

My Heart's Cry

MARCH 28

CARRYING THE CROSS

*"Anyone who does not carry his cross
and follow me cannot be my disciple."*

LUKE 14:27, NIV

Imagine what it would have been like to be Simon, and to have carried the cross of Christ while following Him up Calvary.

What would it have been like to have shared in the humiliation of rejection as He was cast out of the city?

What would it have been like to have felt the sticky warmth of His blood from the cross on your skin?

What would it have been like to have felt the encroaching horror as the place of execution neared?

What would it have been like to have seen the executioners who stood waiting impassively with hammers in hand?

What would it have been like to have the burden of the cross lifted from your back as someone said, "This is His cross; you're free to go now," and He was nailed to it, not you?

Just Give Me Jesus

THE BLOOD OF JESUS

How much more . . . will the blood of Christ . . .
cleanse our consciences from acts that lead to death.

HEBREWS 9:14, NIV

As you look around, what "fruit" do you see others bringing to the place of sacrifice instead of humbly approaching God through the blood of His Son? The "fruit" of

religious activity,

good works,

morality,

or philanthropy?

Many people do not want to come to the place of sacrifice, the cross of Jesus Christ, because it intensifies the conviction of their own sin and judgment and is a reminder that heaven's gate is closed to sinners. God warns that "a man is not justified by observing the law," (Gal. 2:16, NIV) because "without the shedding of blood there is no forgiveness" of sin (Heb. 9:22, NIV). So humble yourself, come to the cross, and thank God for the blood of Jesus that is sufficient to forgive any and all sin.

God's Story

CLOTHED IN HIS RIGHTEOUSNESS

And when they crucified Him,
they divided His garments, casting lots for them
to determine what every man should take.

MARK 15:24, NKJV

When Jesus finally arrived at the place of execution around nine o'clock in the morning, if His treatment followed standard procedure in those days, He was stripped of all His clothes. Possibly He was allowed to retain a loincloth.

Yet because Jesus was stripped "naked," you and I can be clothed! The Bible tells us that all of our righteousness, including the very best things we ever do, are so permeated with sin and selfishness that they are like filthy rags in God's sight (Isa. 64:6). But at the cross, Jesus gave us His perfect, spotless robe of righteousness and took our filthy garments of sin in exchange (Phil. 3:9). On Judgment Day, you and I will be dressed in His righteousness before God because He wore the filthy garments of our sin. We will be clothed because He was stripped!

Just Give Me Jesus

MORE TO LIFE

"I have come that they may have life,
and that they may have it more abundantly."

JOHN 10:10, NKJV

There is more to life . . .
than being healthy,
than being happy,
than being problem free,
than being comfortable,
than feeling good,
than getting what we want,
than being healed.
There is more to life even *than living!*

And the "more to life" is the development of our faith to the extent that our very lives display God's glory!

Jesus does not protect those He loves from bad things but uses bad things to fulfill His greater plan. He is glad, not that we suffer, but that we have the opportunity to grow in our faith and display His glory, which is the fulfillment of the very purpose for our existence. Don't settle for less than more!

Why?

April

The power that produces blessing
comes through brokenness.

HE WILL FORGIVE YOU

"Forgive us our debts, as we forgive our debtors."

MATTHEW 6:12, NKJV

Jesus, the Lamb of God, God's own Son, was sacrificed on the altar of a wooden Roman cross.

Normally, crucifixion victims cursed and screamed obscenities and even passed into unconsciousness from the initial pain. Jesus reacted in a stunningly different way—He prayed, "Father, forgive them, for they do not know what they are doing" (Luke 23:34, NIV). Fifty days later when Peter preached at Pentecost, Jesus' prayer was answered when some of the very men who crucified Him repented of their sins, placed their faith in Him, and were baptized in His Name!

If God could forgive the men who nailed His Son to the cross, why do you think He won't forgive you?

Just Give Me Jesus

JESUS UNDERSTANDS

I will pour . . . on the inhabitants of Jerusalem
the Spirit of grace and supplication;
then they will look on Me whom they pierced.
ZECHARIAH 12:10, NKJV

Hymn writers and artists have conveyed to us a picture of Jesus hanging on a cross on a hill far away. In fact, the place of execution was just outside the city gate, beside the main road leading into Jerusalem. And those to be crucified were only raised two to eighteen inches above the ground. That meant all the dignity and modesty and purity of Jesus' physical person was stripped away and He was left naked to die in searing, scorching heat, writhing and groaning in agony, at virtually eye level with those who passed by on their way to and from the city.

In their rush to get to the temple area in time to purchase a lamb for sacrifice, did the pilgrims preparing for Passover *even notice* the Lamb that God was sacrificing for their sin? As Jesus poured out His life, people must have passed by without a glance.

In a small way, are you pouring out your life for those who don't notice? Jesus understands.

Just Give Me Jesus

FORGIVENESS—AN ACT OF WORSHIP

"Father, forgive them,
for they do not know what they are doing."

LUKE 23:34, NIV

If Jesus forgave those who nailed Him to the cross, and if God forgives you and me, how can you withhold your forgiveness from someone else? How can you withhold your forgiveness from *yourself?* If God says, "I forgive you," then the only appropriate response is to say, "God, thank You. I don't deserve it, but I accept it. And to express my gratitude, I, in turn, forgive that person who has sinned against me."

We forgive others, not because they deserve it, *but because He deserves it!* The only reason we have to forgive is that He commands us to, and our obedience gives us opportunity to say to Him, "Thank You for forgiving me. I love You." Our forgiveness of others then becomes an act of worship that we would not enter into except for Who He is and for the overwhelming debt of love we owe Him.

Just Give Me Jesus

CHANGING YOUR DESTINY

Jesus answered him, "I tell you the truth,
today you will be with me in paradise."

LUKE 23:43, NIV

Even in the blackness of hate and evil swirling around the cross, the love of God broke through like the rays of the sun on a stormy day. That love shone down on the two thieves crucified on each side of Jesus. Their agony and fury boiled over and spewed out in a venom of curses and taunts.

But one of the thieves grew quieter and quieter, until finally he rebuked his partner in crime, "We are punished justly, . . . but this man has done nothing wrong." And then, in one of the most moving conversion scenes in human history, the thief turned his face toward Jesus and pleaded in humble faith, "Jesus, remember me when you come into your kingdom." And Jesus turned his face toward the thief and promised, "I tell you the truth, today you will be with me in paradise." In the twinkling of an eye, that thief changed his eternal destiny; he passed from death to life.

Just Give Me Jesus

GOD'S COMFORT

Blessed be the . . . God of all comfort,
who comforts us in all our tribulation.

2 CORINTHIANS 1:3-4, NIV

How could Mary bear to watch her Son tortured? Yet how could she tear herself away?

Her entire body must have quivered as though from an electric shock as she heard Jesus calling to her from the cross. Surely her breath caught as she strained to hear His words, yet He spoke clearly, "'Dear woman, here is your son,' and to the disciple [John], 'Here is your mother.' From that time on, this disciple took her into his home" (John 19:26–27, NIV). And somehow, even with the horror of the scene before her, and the weight of agony pressing against her chest, she knew everything was going to be all right. She didn't understand, but in the midst of the anguish only a mother knows as her heart is shattered by the pain of her child, a quiet peace must have stolen its way within when God spoke directly and personally to her from the cross. God had singled her out, He had noticed her, He had cared for her, and she was comforted.

Just Give Me Jesus

BECAUSE HE LIVES

"I am the good shepherd.
The good shepherd gives His life for the sheep."

JOHN 10:11, NKJV

Real meaning to your life is found in the glorious dawn of God's story, which breaks into full revelation in the Person of Jesus Christ. What an astounding truth! What a life-changing message!

Because He emptied Himself of all but love, you can be filled.

Because His body was broken, your life can be whole.

Because He was forsaken, you will never be alone.

Because He was buried, you can be raised.

Because He reached down to you, you don't have to work your way up to Him.

Because His promises are always true, you can have hope!

Praise God for just giving us Jesus!

God's Story

APRIL 7

THE EXCHANGE

*By grace you have been saved through faith,
and that not of yourselves; it is the gift of God,
not of works, lest anyone should boast.*

EPHESIANS 2:8–9, NKJV

On the hill of Golgotha, when Jesus was stripped of His physical clothes, the execution squad of soldiers divided what little He had between them—His belt, sandals, and other things. But when it came to His beautifully woven inner garment, they decided that instead of tearing it into four pieces, they would gamble for it. So while Jesus hung slightly above them, groaning in excruciating pain, they callously ignored Him and tossed the dice. (John 19:23–24)

People today still toss the dice for the robe of His righteousness. While coldly ignoring His death on the cross, they gamble for His "robe" by betting their eternal lives on the chance that they can earn acceptance with God through their religiosity, or their sincerity, or their morality. But the only way to obtain it is to exchange your sin for it at the cross.

Just Give Me Jesus

HEAVEN IS REAL

"The angel who talked with me had a measuring rod
of gold to measure the city, its gates and its walls."
REVELATION 21:15, NIV

In Revelation 21 the apostle John describes
the glimpse he was given into God's heavenly home.
My Father's House is real! It is not:

an abstract idea

or a small child's fantasy

or an artist's concept of celestial beauty

or a musician's theme for a symphony

or a fearful person's imaginative escape from harm.

It is the only true home that will keep you and your
loved ones happy, healthy, and safe—forever!

The angel who took John on a guided tour
literally measured the dimensions of Heaven,
emphasizing that it is indeed a literal, specific,
physical, actual place. Heaven is real!

Heaven: My Father's House

APRIL 9

NEVER SEPARATED FROM GOD

"I and My Father are one."

JOHN 10:30, NKJV

"My God, my God, why have you forsaken me?" (Matt. 27:46, NIV) The words came from the cracked lips and the crushed heart of God's Son as His tortured body and fevered mind were pushed to the outer limits of endurance. For the first time in eternity, the Father and Son were actually separated. They were separated by all of your sins and my sins, which came between Them.

Even when Jesus had been alone in a crowd, or alone on a mountainside, or alone on the lake He had never truly been *alone!* His Father had always been with Him. He and His Father were so close they were One. To be separated was a spiritual death that was worse than a living nightmare. *It was hell!*

No one on this side of hell will ever know the loneliness Jesus endured on the cross—in your place and mine. When we claim the Lamb as our own sacrifice for sin, we will never be separated from God, because Jesus was.

Just Give Me Jesus

A PATTERN TO LIVE BY

Six days you shall labor and do all your work,
but the seventh day is a Sabbath to the LORD your God.

EXODUS 20:9–10, NIV

Life on Planet Earth is fast becoming a rat race, and a mad scramble to get ahead that is leaving brokenness everywhere. We desperately need a pattern to live by that will enable us to live our lives successfully. Such a pattern already exists; it was set at the dawn of Creation by God Himself. But we are not following the Creator's directions.

Our twenty-four-hour day is based on the earth's rotation on its axis. Our twelve-month years are based on the revolution of our planet around the sun. But the only basis for the seven-day week that is used worldwide as a pattern for humanity's lifestyle is the Creator's example: "By the seventh day God had finished the work he had been doing; so on the seventh day he rested from all his work" (Gen. 2:2, NIV). While God's week included rest on the seventh day, it also involved work for six days straight, giving us a pattern for the discipline of our lives. How close does the pattern of your life follow His?

God's Story

JESUS REVEALED IN US

Those who suffer according to
God's will should commit themselves to their
faithful Creator and continue to do good.

1 PETER 4:19, NIV

If our kids always behave
and our boss is always pleased
and our home is always orderly
and our bodies always feel good
and we are patient and kind and thoughtful and
happy and loving, others shrug because they're
capable of being that way too. On the other hand, if
we have a splitting headache,
the kids are screaming,
the phone is ringing,
the supper is burning,
yet we are still patient, kind, thoughtful, happy, and
loving, the world sits up and takes notice. The
world knows that kind of behavior is not natural.
It's supernatural. And others see Jesus revealed in us.

Just Give Me Jesus

"IT IS FINISHED"

He said, "It is finished!"
And bowing His head, He gave up His spirit.
JOHN 19:30, NKJV

After nine hours of standing on His feet, after being scourged, slapped, and manhandled, after six hours of hanging on the cross, the average person would have barely had enough life and breath left to even whisper. But Jesus, the Lamb of God, with life still fully flowing through His body, shouted out in a clear, ringing, triumphant voice, "It is finished." The price for our redemption had been paid! The sacrifice for our sin had been made! Sin was forgiven! Guilt was atoned for! Eternal life was now offered! Heaven has been opened! *It is finished!*

You don't have to do more good works than bad works.

You don't have to go to church every time the door opens.

You don't have to climb the stairs to some statue.

You don't have to be religious.

You don't even have to be good!

It is finished! The price has been paid!

Just Give Me Jesus

LIGHT REIGNS OVER DARKNESS

The light shines in the darkness,
but the darkness has not understood it.

JOHN 1:5, NIV

When you and I live lives that reflect Jesus, His light in us reveals the darkness of sin and rebellion and ignorance in the world around us. This may begin to explain why your old friends have rejected you or your coworkers avoid you or your neighbors shun you. If they are living in darkness, the light in you makes them uncomfortable.

They may not be able to "see" God or others or themselves clearly, but they see well enough to get along in life.

When a person who belongs to Jesus Christ lives a life that reflects:

His integrity and morality and purity,

His holiness and righteousness and truthfulness,

His goodness and godliness and grace,

the light of his or her life can cause others to react with spontaneous rejection. But be encouraged! The Light not only reveals the darkness, it also reigns over it.

Just Give Me Jesus

APRIL 14

ARE YOU SAVED?

He who did not spare his own Son, . . .
how will he not also, . . . give us all things?
ROMANS 8:32, NIV

Jesus hung on the cross for three hours, wracked with white-hot physical pain, crushed by the weight of guilt and shame and sin that was ours but became His. Suddenly, the birds stopped chirping, the breeze stopped blowing, and everything became deathly still as darkness—pitch-black darkness—descended. The cries that could be heard were no longer just coming from the victims on the crosses but from the bystanders as they cowered, then fled in panic. Even the hardened soldiers must have shuddered at the supernatural power and anger that permeated the atmosphere.

The eerie darkness that descended was not just nature feeling sorry for the Creator who was nailed to the altar of the cross. It was the very judgment of God for your sins and mine.

Your sin has been judged at the cross, so you can be saved from judgment. Are you saved?

Just Give Me Jesus

WITHOUT CHRIST

"Whoever serves me must follow me;
and where I am, my servant also will be."

JOHN 12:26, NIV

Jesus encouraged His disciples by promising, "where I am, my servant also will be." There is nothing in this world that I desire more than the presence of Jesus in my life.

Nothing . . .

> not houses or honors or health,
> not cars or careers or children,
> not money or marriage or ministry,
> not fame or family or freedom,
> not promotion or pleasures or position,
> not strength or success,
> not ability or achievement,
> not even love or life itself.

Nothing!

What would it be like not to have Christ in your life? I think that it would be hell—literally.

My Heart's Cry

STAND UP FOR JESUS

Joseph of Arimathea asked Pilate for the body of Jesus.
JOHN 19:38, NIV

Because Jesus had just been executed as a criminal and an enemy of Rome, Joseph's request was exceedingly bold. As a prominent member of the religious community, he ran the risk of provoking not only Pilate but also the other Jewish leaders.

Joseph's action was especially astounding since previously he had been so timid and fearful of the opinions of others that he had kept his belief in Jesus as the Messiah a secret. Now, however, he came out of the closet and "with Pilate's permission, he came and took the body." Even more astonishing, "he was accompanied by Nicodemus, the man who earlier had visited Jesus at night" (John 19:38–39, NIV).

The Father's heart must have been deeply moved to see these two fearful, prideful Jewish men throw caution to the wind. They had been silent when they should have spoken. But no more! Now they were standing up for Jesus!

Just Give Me Jesus

GOD REACHES DOWN TO MAN

*"I am the way, the truth, and the life.
No one comes to the Father except through Me."*

JOHN 14:6, NKJV

Karl Barth, one of the twentieth century's premier theologians, said that all religion is man reaching up to God in his own way, according to his own terms, on his own merit, in his own strength. Christianity alone is God reaching down to man.

All non-Judeo-Christian religions are an expression of man's defiance of God, including His way, His will, and His work. If you ask most people today why they think God will let them into heaven, they will say something like, "I try to be good. I go to church. I'm not perfect, but I believe God will weigh my good deeds against my bad deeds, and I hope the good outweighs the bad. If it does, He will let me into heaven." It is man's pride that believes God somehow owes him a heavenly home or eternal life as a reward for good deeds or extra effort or earnest sincerity. But heaven cannot be earned or deserved or bought, which is why God has reached down and just given us Jesus!

God's Story

THE TOMB WAS EMPTY!

Christ died and rose and lived again, that He
might be Lord of both the dead and the living.

ROMANS 14:9, NKJV

Early Sunday morning, in the inky blackness before dawn, soldiers stood guard over Christ's tomb. Knowing that to go to sleep on duty was an offense punishable by death, the highly trained unit remained alert. Their lives depended on it.

Suddenly, "there was a violent earthquake." Almost simultaneously, the predawn darkness was split by a light so brilliant it looked like a laser of lightning! The "lightning" took the shape of an angel who seemed to reach from heaven to earth. Against the inky blackness of the night the terrifyingly awesome being fearlessly descended, walked over to the stone that blocked the tomb's entrance, flicked it away as though it were dust, and then sat on it! And the gaping hole where the stone had been, revealed there was nothing inside the tomb! *The tomb was empty!*

Just Give Me Jesus

OVERCOMING OBSTACLES

*[The women] asked each other, "Who will
roll the stone away from the entrance of the tomb?"*

MARK 16:3, NIV

The women who had been so faithfully
vigilant at the cross during the long hours of Jesus'
suffering returned together first thing Sunday
morning to complete the embalming process that
Joseph and Nicodemus had hastily done late Friday
afternoon.

Their voices could be heard on the brisk early
morning air as they discussed the problem of how
they would roll the stone away. They knew it would
be impossible for them to accomplish, even if all of
them pushed together. What stone, what *obstacle* is
ahead of you that you think you can't move or get
around, that blocks you from fulfilling your
commitment to the Lord? Is it the stone of financial
limitations? practical inexperience? physical weakness?

If we steadfastly cling to our faith in Him,
persevering in our commitment to Him, He will roll
away the stones for us!

Just Give Me Jesus

HE WANTS TO BE YOUR LIFE

No eye has seen, no ear has heard, no mind has conceived what God has prepared for those who love him.

1 CORINTHIANS 2:9, NIV

One of the pictures in John Bunyan's *Pilgrim's Progress* is of a man bending double from his waist, sorting through a can of garbage, carefully extracting the little bits of tinsel he finds there. Behind him is standing an angel who is offering him a solid gold crown studded with precious jewels, but the man is so engrossed in the garbage he never notices the angel.

When we get to heaven, will you and I be ashamed of our preoccupation with "garbage" in this life—garbage that prevented us from dying to our desire for it, turning around, leaving it all behind, and reaching out for what God wanted to give us? Why is it that we seem to cling so tightly to what we want, and in the process lose what God wants us to have? God wants us to have power and blessing and glory. But you don't obtain it by *adding* Jesus to your life—He has to *be* your life!

My Heart's Cry

THE GRAVE CLOTHES

*"Blessed are those who have not seen
and yet have believed."*

JOHN 20:29, NIV

Upon hearing the news of the empty tomb, Peter and John ran to see for themselves. Peter confronted the evidence, but he was confused. At that instant, he must have been angrier than ever. He must have surmised that the enemies of Jesus who had dared to crucify Him, had now taken the body for who knew what purpose!

John quietly looked around. He noticed that the grave clothes were totally unlike those of Lazarus, which had been just a pile of stinking rags by the time Martha had finished unwrapping him. These grave clothes were lying, not as though someone had removed them from the body, but as though the body were still inside! It must have gradually dawned on him that the grave clothes looked like an empty cocoon! They looked as though the body had just evaporated up through them! *Then John knew!* (John 20:8). The body hadn't evaporated. Jesus had risen from the dead!

Just Give Me Jesus

FACING DEATH WITHOUT FEAR

We, according to His promise, look for new heavens and a new earth in which righteousness dwells.

2 PETER 3:13, NKJV

For the past thirteen years I have traveled all over the world in response to invitations to give out God's Word. There have been times, such as my first visit to India, when I have started out by climbing onto the plane with my stomach churning, my knees knocking, and my heart fibrillating—terrified because I was not sure where I was going, or who would meet me at the journey's end. But what a difference there has been in my attitude when I have had the opportunity for a second visit to that same place. I have left home with peace in my heart because I knew where I was going and who would meet me at the journey's end. In the same way, the prospect of death can fill you and me with terror and dread—unless we know where we are going. Knowing as much as we can about our final destination, and Who will meet us at the end of life's journey, takes the fear out of getting there.

Heaven: My Father's House

THE CROSS OF OBEDIENCE

*"If anyone would come after me, he must
deny himself and take up his cross and follow me."*

MATTHEW 16:24, NIV

Are you repulsed by the thought of crucifixion? I am. But I also know that when I look into the eyes of Jesus, I see a cross! And He has said to me, "Anne, if you want to be My disciple, if you want to follow Me, you must deny yourself, take up your cross and follow Me. Because if you want to save your life, you're going to lose it in the end. If you choose to lose your life for Me, you will find it. For what good will it do you if you gain the whole world, yet forfeit your soul?" (Matt. 16:24–26, paraphrased).

The cross that Jesus commands you and me to carry is the cross of submissive obedience to the will of God, even when His will includes suffering and hardship and things we don't want to do. It is a willingness to totally, absolutely, irrevocably, and finally yield our lives to Him because we want what He wants more than what we want.

Just Give Me Jesus

BLESSING THROUGH BROKENNESS

"The man who loves his life will lose it, while the man
who hates his life in this world will keep it for eternal life."

JOHN 12:25, NIV

What is your reaction to that verse? Jesus is the One Who died for *you and me!* Surely He's not saying you and I *must die for Him!* Death is a pretty big stretch from your daily prayer, "God, bless me indeed," isn't it? And it's not nearly as full of wonder and excitement, and if we're honest, personal profit. God wants to bless you and me even more than we could think to ask, but the power that produces the blessing comes through brokenness and death. And not just any death, but death by crucifixion.

Crucifixion is the result of our decision to yield ourselves to God as He allows various pressures and problems and pain into our lives. They are used to put us to death that we might be raised to an abundant, Spirit-filled life. And remember—after the cross comes the resurrection and the glory!

My Heart's Cry

APRIL 25

LOVE FORGIVES AND FORGETS

Love each other deeply,
because love covers over a multitude of sins.

1 PETER 4:8, NIV

King Solomon wisely admonished, "He who covers over an offense promotes love, but whoever repeats the matter separates close friends" (Prov. 17:9, NIV). One of the definitions for love given in the New Testament is that, "Love does not delight in evil. . . . It always protects" (1 Cor. 13:6–7, NIV).

One of the greatest failures in the Bible was the apostle Peter. His most notorious moment of sin was when, after vowing that he would die for Jesus, he actually denied ever having known Him. And he denied Him not just once but three times. Yet God, in His mercy and grace, restored Peter so completely that he was given a prominent leadership position within the early church, opening the door of opportunity for the Gentiles to receive the gospel. And Peter, who understood the shame of failure and the humiliation of sin, encouraged Christians to "love each other deeply, because love covers over a multitude of sins."

God's Story

GOD'S EXPECTATIONS

I can do all things through Christ
who strengthens me.

PHILIPPIANS 4:13, NKJV

I was once sitting in an audience when the speaker asked, "What do you think God expects of you?" I mentally ticked off a list of things I thought God expected of me: obedience, faithfulness, holiness, love, service. To my astonishment, the speaker went on to say, "All God ever expects of you is failure!" I wanted to raise my hand and say, "I can do that! I can live up to the expectations of God! I know I can fail!" But then the speaker added, "However, He has given you the Holy Spirit so that you need never fail." Right! Without Christ I can do nothing, but in Him I can do all things!

The difference between strength and weakness, righteousness and wickedness, success and failure, is Jesus—the Holy Spirit—in me.

God's Story

THE ARK OF SAFETY

The wages of sin is death, but the gift of God
is eternal life in Christ Jesus our Lord.

ROMANS 6:23, NKJV

"And the Lord said unto Noah, 'Come thou and all thy house into the ark; for thee have I seen righteous before me in this generation.'"

The offer God extended to Noah was an invitation to be saved from the judgment that was coming. God has also told you and me that judgment is coming—physical death that ushers us into eternity, where our sin has condemned us to hell. Hell is a place of intense, unending physical suffering, darkness, dissatisfaction, and worst of all, separation from the One for Whom we were created. (Matt. 13:49–50)

At the same time God warns us that judgment is coming, He issues an invitation to come into the Ark He has provided as the means of salvation from it. Jesus Christ is the Ark in which we hide, our Savior from the storm of God's coming judgment. Have you accepted His invitation to "come in"?

God's Story

HE BECAME SIN FOR US

He made Him who knew no sin to be sin for us,
that we might become the righteousness of God in Him.

2 CORINTHIANS 5:21, NKJV

The spiritual suffering Jesus endured on the cross is not as easily recognizable as His physical and emotional suffering, but it was by far the worst suffering of all. We first glimpse it when Jesus was stripped of His robe and left to hang virtually naked before the world. The emotional shame and humiliation would have been acute for any dignified Jewish rabbi. Yet it wouldn't even have warranted an honorable mention alongside the spiritual humiliation He endured as He was spiritually stripped of His robe of righteousness in God's eyes.

Christ didn't just take our sins upon Himself, He *became* those sins for us. Imagine how dirty and vile and evil and guilty and *ashamed* Jesus must have felt as He hung there before a holy God with our sins exposed as *though they were His!* Would you thank Him for bearing your sin—so that you can wear His righteousness?

Just Give Me Jesus

A MARRIAGE TRIANGLE

Do not be yoked together with unbelievers. For what do
righteousness and wickedness have in common?

2 CORINTHIANS 6:14, NIV

One of God's principles for marriage is that those who have established a right relationship with God through faith in Jesus Christ are not to marry those who are not in a right relationship with God. The reason for this principle was explained logically by Amos when he said, "Do two walk together unless they have agreed to do so?" (Amos 3:3, NIV) For someone who has real faith in God to marry, or "walk with," another person who is in rebellion against God would mean a lifetime of compromise on everything from how to spend time and money, to setting priorities and standards. If there is no basic agreement on an issue as significant as a person's relationship with God, then there can be no agreement on lesser issues, and a compromise would have to be made to preserve the marriage.

So . . . make your marriage a triangle, with Jesus Christ at the apex. As you and your spouse grow closer to God you will grow closer together.

God's Story

HE'S ALIVE!

*That you may know . . . the exceeding greatness
of His power . . . which He worked in Christ when
He raised Him from the dead.*

EPHESIANS 1:18–20, NKJV

God the Father split history in two when He flexed the divine, eternal muscle of His will and exerted His power on His Son's behalf! How He must have eagerly anticipated and rejoiced in the vindication and resurrection of His Son! His power was so mightily tremendous that Jesus was:

Raised up from the dead!

Raised up without our sin!

Raised up to life!

Raised up through the walls of the tomb!

Raised up past the guards!

Raised up through all His invisible enemies!

Raised up to a position of authority over the entire universe!

Raised up to be seated at the right hand of God!

Jesus was raised up! He's alive!

Just Give Me Jesus

May

Nothing is too small for God's attention.

A FRIEND OF GOD

Are You not our God, who drove out
the inhabitants of this land . . . and gave it to
the descendants of Abraham Your friend forever?

2 CHRONICLES 20:7, NKJV

Recently I was invited to address a group of professional women golfers the night before the U.S. Women's Open. I was struck by the intensity of their focus as they pursued their goal of competing in and winning the golf tournament. Their entire lives revolved around their one purpose—of being the best golfers they could be. I told them I also had a similar sense of purpose that dictated where I went, how I spent my time and who I interacted with. For approximately the past twenty-five years, I have nailed down what I believe to be God's purpose for my life, and I have sought to achieve it. Simply stated, it is to increasingly grow in my personal knowledge of God as I follow Him in a life of faith.

I want to know God today better than I knew Him yesterday. I want to know Him better next year than I do this year. I want to know Him until one day, like Abraham, God refers to me as His friend!

My Heart's Cry

GOD IS EVERYWHERE

Where can I go from Your Spirit?
Or where can I flee from Your presence?

PSALM 139:7. NKJV

You and I can only be in one place at any given time because we are bound by space. Right now I am at my desk in my home. As much as I might like to be with my parents four hours away or with my son in California or with my daughters in Texas, I can only be in one place, and for now it's right here, in my study, working at my computer. But God can be everywhere at once. God, in all of His fullness, is present

with pastors in Bosnia trying to keep the unity of the Spirit in the midst of generations of division,

with Christians in Rwanda seeking to glorify God in the midst of an earthly hell,

with Christians in South Africa seeking to love one another equally,

with me, as I write this book,

and *with you* as you read it!

Where did you think God was not? God is everywhere!

God's Story

AUTHENTIC SHEPHERDS

*"The man who enters by the gate
is the shepherd of his sheep."*

JOHN 10:2, NIV

The winter sheepfolds were located in the barren, rocky Judean hills. Each one was used by several shepherds who kept their flocks in the fold during the night for safety. The fold would have had high stone walls accessed by one strong, wooden door. It had no roof. One of the shepherds would act as the watchman at the door, guarding against thieves, wild animals, and anything else that might harm the sheep. In the morning, the authentic shepherds of the sheep would come to the door and identify themselves. The watchman would open the door, then each shepherd would call out his own sheep by name. One by one, his particular sheep would follow him out to the Judean hills.

You and I, as God's "sheep," can determine the authenticity of the shepherds by their approach to us. The criterion for the authentic shepherd is that he or she always approaches through the door of God's Word.

My Heart's Cry

MAY 4

YOU CAN KNOW GOD

*You will seek the LORD your God,
and you will find Him if you seek Him
with all your heart and with all your soul.*

DEUTERONOMY 4:29, NKJV

If Adam knew God as a beloved Father,
if Eve knew Him as the original Homemaker,
if Noah knew Him as the Refuge from the storm,
if Abraham knew Him as a Friend,
if Moses knew Him as the Redeemer,
if Rahab knew Him as the gracious Savior,
if David knew Him as his Shepherd,
if Elijah knew Him as the Almighty,
if Daniel knew Him as the Lion Tamer,
if Mary Magdalene knew Him as the Bondage
    Breaker,
if Martha knew Him as the Promise Keeper,
if Lazarus knew Him as the Resurrection and
    the Life,
if John knew Him as the glorious King upon
    the throne,
surely you and I can know Him too!

Just Give Me Jesus

NOTHING'S TOO SMALL FOR GOD

The LORD is righteous in all His way,
gracious in all his works.

PSALM 145:17, NKJV

God created snowflakes, no two of which are alike. He created a sponge-like pad between the head of a woodpecker and its bill to absorb the shock when the bird strikes a tree. He created nerve cells that connect the human body to the brain like tiny telephone wires, with messages traveling along them up to three hundred miles per hour!

God is active in small ways in the universe, on our planet, in our bodies, and in our lives! What do you think is so small that it's too small for God to notice?

A small tear?

A small hurt feeling?

A small insult?

A small sin?

A small worry?

Nothing is too small for the Creator's attention and activity!

God's Story

MY MOTHER'S ABIDING JOY

In Your presence is fullness of joy;
at Your right hand are pleasures forevermore.

PSALM 16:11, NKJV

As a teenager growing up, my room in our house was directly over Mother's. At night I could see the lights from her room reflected on the trees outside my window. When I slipped downstairs hoping to talk to her a few minutes, I would find her shapely form bent beside her bed in prayer. It was useless to wait for her to rise because she would be there for hours on end, so I would trudge back up to my room. And no matter how early I awoke in the morning, I would see those lights from her window once again reflected on the trees outside. My mother chose to make abiding in Christ one of the priorities of her life.

Mother's abiding is rooted in a love relationship with Jesus that is the secret of her life. As a result of her abiding, the hallmark of Mother's life is joy. Her face radiates with it! Her eyes sparkle with it! And I'm left to wonder . . . what outward evidence of my inner relationship with Jesus do *my children* see?

My Heart's Cry

THE CITY BUILT BY GOD

*[Abraham] was looking forward to the city
with foundations, whose architect and builder is God.*

HEBREWS 11:10, NIV

About four thousand years ago, Abraham left
Ur of the Chaldees, looking for "the city with
foundations, whose architect and builder is God."
As he followed God in a life of faith, he lived in a
tent that he constantly moved from place to place.
He never settled down. He knew he was just an
alien and a stranger on earth—just a pilgrim passing
through to a great eternal city with foundations.

Can you imagine the thrill that will be Abraham's
when he bursts through the gates of My Father's
House, shouting, "I've found it! I've found what I
have been hoping for! All the days and nights of
wandering and living in tents were worth it. All of
God's promises are true!" All of Abraham's goals and
hopes and dreams—those things that were the
driving motivational forces in his life—had been
focused on his eternal home, and he will not be
disappointed! The city of his dreams is built by God!

Heaven: My Father's House

HIS FAITHFUL SERVANTS

"No servant is greater than his master,
nor is a messenger greater than the one who sent him."

JOHN 13:16, NIV

Jesus is our risen Lord and reigning King! You and I are to serve Him by getting involved in meeting the needs of others simply because He says so! He is Lord! And while we should never forget Who He is, we should also never forget who we are!

You and I are . . .

sinners saved, (1 John 4:16)
blood bought, (Phil. 4:5)
prisoners freed, (Num. 14:13)
glory bound. (Ezra 9:15)

We are not our own. We belong to Him. (2 Cor. 12:9, NKJV)

Our lives no longer are to be lived according to what we want but according to what He says. We are His faithful servants. If you know your place, have you accepted it?

My Heart's Cry

THE SUFFICIENCY OF GOD'S POWER

To Him who is able to do exceedingly abundantly
above all that we ask or think, according to the
power that works in us, . . . be glory.
EPHESIANS 3:20–21, NKJV

The infinite power of the Living Logos of God is adequate for any need you or I will ever have.

We may intellectually grasp the truth that God's power is adequate, but we can never know that by experience if we stay in our comfort zone. If all you ever attempt is what you know you can do yourself, if all your needs seem to be met through someone or something other than God, if you never have any difficulties that are greater than you can bear—how will you know the awesome greatness and personal availability of His infinite power? It's when the Red Sea is before you, the mountains are on one side of you, the desert is on the other side, and you feel the Egyptian army closing in from behind that you experience His power to open up an escape route. He has power to do the supernatural, the unthinkable, the impossible.

Just Give Me Jesus

MAY 10

DISPLAY CASES FOR GOD'S GLOI

*Do you not know that you are the temple of God
and that the Spirit of God dwells in you?*
1 CORINTHIANS 3:16, NKJV

In the Old Testament, the glory of God appeared to the children of Israel as a pillar of cloud by day and a pillar of fire by night as they were led for forty years in the wilderness. On occasion, the glory of God would envelop the tabernacle and later the temple with a golden glory cloud as a manifestation of God's Presence.

But the Bible says God's glory is no longer revealed in a cloudy, fiery pillar; it is no longer revealed in a golden, glowing cloud. The glory of God is within you and me through the Spirit of God, Who indwells us when we receive Jesus Christ by faith as our personal Savior and Lord! You and I are the display cases for God's glory as His living temples.

When others look in your "display case," what do they see?

God's Story

LIKE JESUS

Whom He foreknew, He also predestined
to be conformed to the image of His Son.

ROMANS 8:29, NKJV

Do you ever get frustrated with the habits of sin in your life? I do! Even though I have been to the cross and received forgiveness for all my sin, I still sin. I don't want to. I try not to. I hate sin! But I still sin. The reality of sin is the single most discouraging, defeating, depressing fact in my life. But I can look forward with hope. Because one day, when I get to My Father's House, all of my sin . . .

> my sinful tendencies,
> my sinful thoughts,
> my sinful actions,
> my sinful words
> my sinful feelings . . .

all my sins are going to fall away like a stinking garment that finally drops off and is discarded. What will be left will be the character of Christ that has been developed in me during my life on earth, and I will be like Jesus!

Heaven: My Father's House

DIVERSITY IN MARRIAGE

Put on tender mercies, kindness, humility,
meekness, longsuffering; bearing with one another.
COLOSSIANS 3:12–13, NKJV

My husband likes everything in its place while I never even notice when things are a mess. He is very outgoing, able to recall people's names easily. In contrast, I am almost a recluse and can't even remember the faces of people I've met.

One day, following weeks of tension and fighting triggered by these differences, we began to make a study of the gifts of the Holy Spirit. We recognized our own particular spiritual gifts, and they were totally opposite from each other. This led us to recognize other differences, acknowledge those differences by name, learn to accept them in each other, and then grow to appreciate them for the balance they give to our marriage relationship. I cannot adequately convey the blessing this has been, the peace that has resulted, and the love that has increased between us simply because after years of doing it "my way," we finally followed the Creator's wise directions for diversity in our marriage.

God's Story

RECEIVE WHAT YOU ASK FOR

"I tell you the truth,
my Father will give you whatever you ask in my name."

JOHN 16:23, NIV

Jesus said we are to ask if we want to receive. My mother encouraged me as a little girl to pray specifically. She bought me a small white leather notebook, and in it I carefully recorded my requests. Then, at her instruction, I left a blank line under each one so I could record the date of the answer. In the front of the little book, she penned these words:

> Thou art coming to a King,
> Large petitions with thee bring,
> For His grace and power are such,
> None can ever ask too much!

So feel free to ask! But leave a blank space under your request so you can record the answer! Because Jesus said if we ask we will receive.

My Heart's Cry

GOD KNOWS YOU AND ME

He knows how we are formed,
he remembers that we are dust.

PSALM 103:L14, NIV

God will never expect more from me than the Holy Spirit will do in and through me if I allow Him the freedom.

What a blessed relief to be reminded that God knows me—in fact, He knows me so well He understands that apart from Him I can do nothing.

I don't have to prove myself to God.

I don't have to worry about disappointing God.

I don't have to earn His respect.

I don't have to deserve His blessings.

I don't have to work hard to be accepted.

I don't have to produce a quota.

I don't have to be successful.

He created me in the first place. "He knows how [I] am formed, he remembers that [I] am dust." I am just a little dust person infused with the very breath of God!

Just Give Me Jesus

PLACES OF SPIRITUAL BENEFIT

These commandments . . . are to be upon your hearts.
Impress them on your children.

DEUTERONOMY 6:6-7, NIV

Our homes are to be places of moral, spiritual, social, emotional, and physical benefit. If you think that what you do within the privacy of your own home is your own business, think again! God has made it His business, and you and I will experience serious consequences if we refuse to follow His directions for our homes.

If we do not instruct our children about God and His "Manufacturer's directions" for living, they will develop their own standards and values based on what they feel, what they think, what their friends are doing, and what seems to work—and in one generation we will see the chaos and confusion that result from their "guessing" their way through life. God has given us directions telling us how to live a life that works. If we are to prevent brokenness, our homes should be places of moral and spiritual benefit to those living within them.

God's Story

MAY 16

THE PEARLY GATES

The twelve gates were twelve pearls,
each gate made of a single pearl.
REVELATION 21:21, NIV

Pearls are formed when a small grain of sand becomes embedded in an oyster, irritating it. To soften the irritation, the oyster coats the grain of sand with a smooth layer of what is called "mother of pearl." As long as the oyster can feel the irritation, it continues to coat the sand with layers of pearl. What kind of irritation would have been necessary to form the pearls that make up the gates to our heavenly city when they are so large they can fit into a wall that is *two hundred feet thick?*! It must have been more than just irritation. It must have been horrendous, severe suffering!

I *wonder* . . . are the pearls a reminder, every time you and I enter My Father's House, that we enter only because of the intense suffering and death of God's Son? Do those pearly gates reflect the cross of Jesus Christ? *Heaven: My Father's House*

MORE CONSISTENCY

"Abide in Me, and I in you."

JOHN 15:4, NKJV

The branch is totally, absolutely, completely dependent upon the Vine, not only for fruit, but for life. Whether because of pride or fear or some other reason, we as branches seem to struggle with being totally dependent on the Vine.

In what areas of your life are you acting independently of the Vine? I can usually determine these areas by just checking my prayer life. The items I have not prayed about— the people and problems, the relationships and responsibilities, the activities and attitudes, the schedules and stress, the entertainment and exercise, the pleasures and pastimes, the decisions and dreams, the desires and diets, anything and everything—are those areas of my life where I am not dependent upon Him. If my heart's cry is for more of His fruitfulness, then one of the goals of my life needs to be more consistency in my dependency. Would you make this your goal, too?

My Heart's Cry

WONDER OF WONDERS

*Though your sins are like scarlet,
they shall be as white as snow.*

ISAIAH 1:18, NKJV

In the Old Testament, when a person sinned, he was required to take the very best lamb he could find to the priest at the temple. There, in front of the priest, the sinner would grasp the lamb with both hands and confess his sin. His guilt was transferred to the lamb. The priest would then hand the sinner a knife, and the sinner would kill the lamb so that it was obvious the lamb had died as a result of the sinner's action.

The pervasive misconception today is that since Jesus died as a sacrifice for the sins of the world, then we are all automatically forgiven. But we overlook the vital truth that we must grasp the Lamb with our hands of faith and confess our sins. We then must acknowledge that He was slain for our sins. At that moment, the Lamb becomes our High Priest and offers His own blood on the altar of the cross on our behalf. And, wonder of wonders! God accepts the sacrifice and we are forgiven!

Just Give Me Jesus

GLORY FOLLOWS SUFFERING

*The sufferings of this present time are not worthy to
be compared with the glory which shall be revealed in us.*

ROMANS 8:18, NKJV

Bad things *do happen* to those Jesus loves.
But remember this spiritual principle: Glory follows
suffering, and life follows death.

Miss Audrey Wetherell Johnson was born in
England, educated in Europe, delivered from
agnosticism, and transformed by God's grace into a
gifted Bible teacher and preacher. She answered
God's call to the mission field in China during the
1930s. After years of teaching in a seminary in
Beijing, Miss Johnson was scooped up with other
missionaries and placed in a Japanese concentration
camp for three years of intolerable suffering. Yet
once again we glimpse God's glory when we learn
that Miss Johnson was finally released, came to
America, and began Bible Study Fellowship, an
international ministry that now provides material
for over one million men and women to study
God's Word each week.

If something bad has happened to you, would
you look forward to the glory that IS coming?!

Why?

A RADICAL CHANGE

"Leave your country, your people and your father's household and go to the land I will show you."

GENESIS 12:1. NIV

God promised to bless Abraham, but Abraham would not receive all God had for him unless he claimed it by leaving everything—his familiar surroundings, his comfortable lifestyle, his old friends, his values, his job, his home, and even his family—and set out on a life of faith. God told him, "Leave your country, your people and your father's household and go to the land I will show you." Abraham did not know where God would lead, just that he was to follow. God's command was clear. Abraham was to put God first in his life if he wanted to receive God's blessing.

If Abraham obeyed God by putting Him first and by following His lead for the rest of his life, things would be dramatically different. He must have known that God was not just adding a weekend hobby or an additional commitment to an already busy life. God was describing a radical change!

God's Story

MAY 21

A QUIET MIRACLE

Jesus then took the loaves, gave thanks, and distributed to those who were seated as much as they wanted.

JOHN 6:11, NIV

When Jesus miraculously fed the crowd with five loaves and two fishes, the people weren't just given a snack or a bite to tide them over until they could get a full meal, they "all had enough to eat" (John 6:12, NIV)!

It was such a quiet, unobtrusive miracle—nothing flashy or showy or manipulative or spectacular. There had been no adequate resources to feed so many people at once, yet everyone was not only fed but also filled!

How had He accomplished the miracle? The formula is really quite simple.

The disciples gave it all.

Jesus took it all.

God blessed it all.

Jesus broke it all.

The disciples gave it all.

And the entire multitude was fed!

Just Give Me Jesus

OUR BUILT-IN ALARM SYSTEM

Sanctify the Lord God in your hearts, . . .
having a good conscience, that . . . those who revile
your good conduct . . . may be ashamed.

1 PETER 3:15–16, NKJV

Wrong attitudes have enormous power in our lives. That's why God has placed within each of us a conscience that begins to feel guilty when our attitudes and actions are wrong.

Many of the later-model cars are equipped with theft alarm systems. The more sensitive ones can be annoying to the general public as the least bit of motion by a passerby or the lightest touch to the car body can send off an ear-splitting siren accompanied by flashing lights and honking horn. But that obnoxious sensitivity is purposefully designed to be a protection against unwanted entry.

God has built into each of us an alarm system to warn us of the unwanted entry of sin into our lives. The alarm system is called guilt. Guilt is our friend. Without it we would go on in sin until we were dominated and defeated by it. So . . . heed the alarm and repent of your sin!

God's Story

JESUS FINISHED GOD'S WORK

*"My food . . . is to do the will of him
who sent me and to finish his work."*

JOHN 4:34, NIV

After having walked all morning and talked
with the woman of Samaria for the better part of
the afternoon, Jesus' disciples returned with food,
urging Him to eat. He resisted their urging by
saying, "I have food to eat that you know nothing
about." When the confused disciples wondered
what He meant, He explained, "My food . . . is to do
the will of him who sent me and to finish his work."

In order to finish God's work, Jesus had to keep
His focus and embrace that purpose with a single
heart and mind, lining up all of His priorities
accordingly. The result of finishing His Father's
work would be even more deeply satisfying than
food to a starving man.

If you and I are able to finish God's work, it
will not be an accident. It will be because we have
been focused every minute of every day of every
week of every month of every year of our lives on
God's purpose.

My Heart's Cry

A SHOWCASE FOR GOD'S GLORY

*"You will receive power when the Holy Spirit comes
on you; and you will be my witnesses."*

ACTS 1:8, NKJV

Jesus described the powerful witness of a life that is different when He illustrated it as "the light of the world" (Matt. 5:14). The primary value of light is that it is so different from the darkness. When Jesus then informed His disciples that "you will be my witnesses," it was clear that one primary value of the apostles' witness would lie in the difference of their lives from those who lived around them.

A witness that is lived can be as powerful as one that is spoken. It's not what you say but who you are that catches the attention of those around you—which is one reason God allows grievances, crises, sufferings, injustice, and hardship to come into our lives. Because problems offer us the opportunity to give silent, relevant witness to the difference faith in God can make. The problems enable us to become a showcase so that the world can look into our lives and see the glory of God revealed.

God's Story

THE SWITCH THAT
TURNS ON THE LIGHT

I will sing to the LORD, for he has been good to me.

PSALM 13:2, NIV

King David knew that the secret of victory over adversity was a conscious choice to praise God. Again and again, as he cries out to God in prayer, we hear his choice to praise: "How long must I wrestle with my thoughts and every day have sorrow in my heart? . . . Look on me and answer, O LORD my God. . . . But I will trust in your unfailing love; my heart rejoices in your salvation. I will sing to the LORD, for he has been good to me" (Ps. 13:2–6, NIV). David, hounded by Saul and living as a fugitive for years in a nation where he was the national hero as well as the anointed king, exercised his will to praise God even when he just didn't feel like it.

Praise is the switch that turns on the light of joy in our lives even when it's "dark" outside. And the resulting "light" causes others to see the glory of God in our lives.

My Heart's Cry

ENERGIZED AND STRENGTHENED

We have received, not the spirit of the world,
but the Spirit who is from God.
1 CORINTHIANS 2:12, NKJV

The Holy Spirit Who now lives in you is the same Holy Spirit in Genesis 1 Who hovered over the formless, empty, dark blob of earth that dangled in space. As He powerfully energized and pulsated the atmosphere, He prepared the planet to receive God's Word and be transformed into a place of purpose and beauty that ultimately, in the end, reflected the image of God.

That same Holy Spirit is now powerfully at work in your life, hovering over your heart, preparing you to love God and be fully aware of His love for you. He hovers over your mind, preparing you to understand spiritual things and the truth of His Word. He hovers over your will, preparing you to make decisions that are pleasing to Him. All the power of God—the same power that hung the stars in place and put the planets in their courses and transformed Earth—now resides in you to energize and strengthen you to become the person God created you to be.

Just Give Me Jesus

MAY 27

RUN FROM TEMPTATION!

Flee . . . evil desires.
2 TIMOTHY 2:22, NIV

Eve became dissatisfied with God's will when Satan was able to focus her attention on the one thing God had said she could not have—the forbidden fruit. The temptation intensified because she tolerated it by talking to the Serpent about it.

But the basic problem was not what she said; it was that she said anything at all! As she conversed with the Serpent she got into deeper trouble, because he responded, "You will not surely die" (Gen. 3:4, NIV). That was an absolute contradiction of what God did say! Eve was confronted with Satan's word against God's Word.

Jesus said we are to cut temptation out of our lives by severing ourselves from whatever is causing us to be tempted. (Matt. 5:29–30) The apostle Paul said we should run from it. Nowhere in the Bible does it say we are to *talk* about it! Unless we do our talking with the Lord! So . . . cut it out! And pray while you run from temptation!

God's Story

GOD IS WITH YOU

I trust in your unfailing love;
my heart rejoices in your salvation.

PSALM 13:5, NIV

The apostle John, suffering in exile on Patmos near the end of his life, must have prayed earnestly to be restored to his church and to his ministry. He must have begged God to get him off of the remote island so he could continue preaching and serving as a pastor and evangelist. Yet God didn't answer his prayers. Instead, John related that it was on Patmos that God drew near to him and gave him a vision of the glory of Jesus Christ—a vision he recorded for the encouragement of every generation of believers since that time in the Book of Revelation. Jesus was with him in exile on Patmos!

What is your Patmos? A place where you are seemingly cut off and exiled from ministry and family? Is it a hospital bed? Or a small home with small children? Is it a workplace where you are surrounded by politically correct hostility to Christ?

Then look up! God is with you!

Why?

NATURE'S WITNESS

As long as the earth endures, seedtime and harvest,
cold and heat, summer
and winter, day and night will never cease.

GENESIS 8:21-22, NIV

In spite of the sin and rebellion that God knew lurked in the very next generation of Noah's sons and would increase with every subsequent generation, God committed Himself to spare the earth His previous judgments. While He did not remove the curse He had placed on Planet Earth following Adam and Eve's sin in the Garden, He vowed He would not increase the curse. And He promised that never again would He destroy all life on the planet as He had done during the Flood.

As evidence that He was good and would keep His promise, God pointed to the very cycles in nature. As you and I see the winter snows give way to spring flowers and the summer's heat give way to autumn's briskness, we are reminded that in back of the changes is the God Who never changes.

God's Story

LET GO!

Let us throw off everything that hinders
and the sin that so easily entangles.

HEBREWS 12:1, NIV

Jesus Christ has set you and me free as surely
as He raised Lazarus from the dead, but we have to
take off the grave clothes *and let them go!*

The writer to the Hebrews exhorts us to throw
off the grave clothes and "everything that hinders
and the sin that so easily entangles and let us run
with perseverance the race marked out for us."

Don't wallow in your "whys."

Don't throw a pity-party.

Don't remain in your misery.

Understand that *you may not understand* this
side of heaven.

Trust God to sort it all out in the end.   *Why?*

HEIRS TOGETHER

Husbands, . . . dwell with them with understanding,
giving honor to the wife, as to the weaker vessel,
and as being heirs together of the grace of life.

1 PETER 3:7, NKJV

The Bible clearly teaches there is to be an equality between man and woman, husband and wife. "In the image of God, . . . male and female he created them. God blessed them and said to them, 'Be fruitful and increase in number; fill the earth and subdue it'" (Gen. 1:27–28, NIV).

Dominion over everything was given to the woman as well as to the man. The woman was not inferior to the man; nor was the man greater than the woman. Men and women, husbands and wives, were and are equal. The New Testament reaffirms the principle of equality when it says men and women are "heirs together of the grace of life."

God in His wisdom created man and woman equal in His sight, and this equality is to be reflected in the marriage relationship. Husbands and wives are to give each other respect, appreciation, and understanding as equal partners.

God's Story

June

Jesus is the very heart
of the Almighty God.

NEVER SEPARATED AGAIN

Neither death nor life . . .
nor things present nor things to come, . . .
shall be able to separate us from the love of God.

ROMANS 8:38–39, NKJV

I love the sea. Every summer, I spend as much time there as I am able. I love to see the vast expanse of sky and water. I love to hear the waves crashing on the shore. I love to walk along the beach and feel the sand beneath my feet and the breeze blowing gently in my face. But the sea separates families and friends and entire continents from each other! In Heaven, there will be *nothing* to separate us from each other or from God. Ever!

No hard feelings or hurt feelings,
No misunderstandings or critical spirits,
No divorce or death,
No sickness or weakness,
No dangers or hardships.
Nothing will ever separate us in My Father's House.

Heaven: My Father's House

THE FOCUS OF OUR FAITH

We have access by faith into this grace in which we stand, and rejoice in hope of the glory of God.

ROMANS 5:2, NKJV

Sometimes, when faced with great problems, our tendency is to focus on the *hands* of God— what He has not done for us and what we want Him to do for us—instead of focusing on the *face* of God—simply Who He is. Our depression can deepen through this kind of self-preoccupation. Often, in the midst of great problems, we stop short of the real blessing God has for us, which is a fresh vision of Who He is. When we stop focusing on our problems and on ourselves and focus instead on our almighty and omnipresent God, our problems, as the old hymn promises, "grow strangely dim in the light of His glory and grace."

Have you grown so impatient, wanting your problems solved now, that you are missing the vision of His glory God has for you? Get your eyes off yourself, your problems, your circumstances, and look to the face of Christ!

The Vision of His Glory

HE IS FULLY ABLE

Through him all things were made;
without him nothing was made that has been made.

JOHN 1:3, NIV

———

God is not one of several gods. He is absolutely
supreme over everything! God is greater than creation.
This means there is nothing in my life—

no circumstance or crisis,

no habit or heartache,

no sickness or grief,

nothing visible or invisible—

nothing that is greater than God!

What are you facing that is greater than you are?

A habit?

A person?

A problem?

Praise God for His deity! He is the Creator Who is
in authority over everything, fully able to control
that which not only *seems* but *is* beyond our abilities
to handle.

God's Story

A PROMISE OF HOPE!

The trumpet will sound, the dead will be
raised imperishable, and we will be changed.

2 CORINTHIANS 15:52, NIV

What will it be like on that day when we hear the clarion call of the archangel's trumpet? Quicker than you or I can blink an eye, believers will feel their feet lifting up off the ground, we will be aware of certain changes taking place in our bodies that will enable us to physically live in eternity, and we will look up—into the face of Jesus! We will be swept into the clouds of His glory! And if we can drag our eyes away from His beautiful face, we will see that Jesus is surrounded by our loved ones who had trusted Him by faith and who had been raised from the dead!

Jesus Christ is coming! He is coming! On any day, at any moment, "in the twinkling of an eye . . . at an hour when you do not expect him . . . he who is coming will come and will not delay" (1 Cor. 15:52; Luke 12:40; Heb. 10:37). Now that's a promise that gives us HOPE!

My Heart's Cry

THE EXACT REVELATION OF GOD

In the beginning was the Word,
and the Word was with God, and the Word was God.
He was with God in the beginning.

JOHN 1:1-2, NIV

John's choice of wording in the Greek language is significant. His Greek for "Word," which he emphasized by repeating three times in the first verse, is *logos*, the outward expression of the mind and will that rules the universe.

As we meditate on John's words, we realize that the Logos who was in the beginning with God is a living Person . . . but He is more. He is the living expression of what is on God's mind. But He is more. He is the living expression of what is on God's heart. But He is even more. He is the very heart of the Almighty God of the universe laid bare for all to see!

Do you want to know what is on the mind of God? Then look at Jesus! Do you want to know the will of God? Then look at Jesus! Do you want to know what is in the heart of God? Then look at Jesus! He is the exact revelation of God!

Just Give Me Jesus

GOD TAKES THE INITIATIVE

Who has understood the mind of the LORD,
or instructed him as his counselor?

ISAIAH 40:13, NIV

"Who has understood the mind of the
LORD, or instructed him as his counselor?" The
answer that reverberates through the millenniums
is . . . no one . . . no one. God stands in the august
solitude of Himself. When He acts, it is because He
Himself has taken the initiative and made the
decision to do so.

God took the initiative
> to create the universe: "And God said . . . ,"
> to create man: "Let us make man in our
> image . . . ,"
> to create woman: "I will make a helper. . . ."

And God took the initiative to send His Son to
be our Savior.

How unbelievably awesome is the One Who
created everything!

God's Story

BUILT TO LAST

The wall of the city had twelve foundations, and on
them were the names of the twelve apostles of the Lamb.

REVELATION 21:14, NIV

My Father's House is a home built to last, not
just for a lifetime, but forever! As John continued to
gaze on the spectacular vision God gave him, he
described Heaven as a city with foundations: "The
wall of the city had twelve foundations, and on
them were the names of the twelve apostles of the
Lamb. . . . The foundations of the city walls were
decorated with every kind of precious stone" (Rev.
21:14, 19). The walls of Heaven are actually built
on twelve foundations, each one decorated with a
different gem. In addition to the spectacular beauty
that is implied, we can be assured that Heaven is
eternal and unshakable. It's permanent!

Our world is a very unstable place. We can
never be certain of the future for ourselves or for the
next generation. The fear and apprehension of
what's around the corner of our lives can be
paralyzing. But when we get to Heaven, we will be
certain and sure of absolute, total, infinite stability.
Heaven is built to last!

Heaven: My Father's House

JUNE 8

THE WAY UP IS DOWN

He humbled himself and became obedient to death—
even death on a cross!

PHILIPPIANS 2:8, NIV

What opinion do you have of yourself? Because of the lofty position you hold, at least in your own eyes, what service do you think is degrading and "beneath" you? Washing dishes? Baby-sitting children? Visiting prisoners?

The apostle Paul, writing from a Roman prison cell, exhorted you and me to have the same attitude of Jesus, "Who, being in very nature God, did not consider equality with God something to be grasped, but made himself nothing, taking the very nature of a servant, being made in human likeness. And being found in appearance as a man, he humbled himself and became obedient to death— even death on a cross!" (Phil. 2:6–8, NIV) How repulsive and prideful to think anything—any job, any person, any position, any service, any task, any place—is beneath you and me when Jesus, Lord of glory, Creator of the universe, left heaven's throne and took upon Himself the form of a servant! The way up is down!

My Heart's Cry

LOOK TO JESUS!

*The wages of sin is death, but the gift of God
is eternal life in Christ Jesus our Lord.*

ROMANS 6:23, NIV

The wonderful good news of the Gospel was shouted out so clearly by the apostle Paul that it still resounds today: The wages of sin is physical death and spiritual deadness as well. BUT the gift of God is eternal life, spiritual life, abundant life through faith in Jesus Christ, the Living Word of God.

What did you think you had to add to your existence in order to experience real life?

Increasing your investment portfolio?

Traveling to more exotic destinations?

Possessing the latest car or computer?

Achieving public recognition?

Reaching your professional goal?

Wearing the trendiest fashion?

If you want lasting purpose and meaning and satisfaction and fulfillment and peace and hope and joy and abundant life that lasts forever, *look to Jesus!*

Just Give Me Jesus

AN ADDED DIMENSION

I have rejoiced in the way of Your testimonies,
as much as in all riches.
PSALM 119:14, NKJV

While God's Word is not like a magic wand, it does have the power, when applied by the Holy Spirit, to give a new dimension to your mind and emotions and also to your will. Have you lacked the willpower to stay on a diet, conquer a bad habit, or develop disciplines necessary for character? Until I began to receive God's Word daily, I never had the willpower to get up early in the morning for a time of prayer. I lacked what has been called "blanket victory"—victory over those blankets in the early-morning hours! But God has given my will an added dimension so that I am now able to do what I formerly could not.

Does your life feel confined? Do you sometimes have the uneasy feeling that something is missing, that there must be something more to life than what you are experiencing? That you are not fulfilling your potential? Then open your heart and mind to God's Word and ask Him to give your life an added dimension.

God's Story

DRASTIC PRUNING

"He cuts off every branch in me that bears no fruit."
JOHN 15:2, NIV

The fruit of the vineyard is only borne in abundance on tender, fairly new growth. As the wood of a branch gets older, it tends to get harder. So even though a branch is living and is connected to the vine, it can become barren. Still leaving the branch connected to the vine, the gardener cuts back the old, hard wood, forcing it into new growth that will produce fruit instead of just more wood and leaves. In fact, there are times when he cuts the branch back so drastically all that is left of it is the connection to the vine.

Jesus described this drastic pruning in a believer's life when He explained that the Gardener "cuts off every branch in me that bears no fruit." There are times when God cuts everything out of our lives except our relationship with Jesus. He forces us to pay attention to our relationship with Him because that's all we have. And in the process, our "connection" to the Vine is enlarged and fruit is produced.

My Heart's Cry

JUNE 12

INVITE JESUS INTO YOUR MARRIAGE

A wedding took place at Cana in Galilee.
Jesus' mother was there, and Jesus and his disciples
had also been invited to the wedding.
JOHN 2:1–2, NIV

Jesus accepted the invitation to a wedding!

Have you invited Jesus to participate in your marriage? Marriage was His idea. He gave the basic ground rules for it. He knows how it works best. And He longs to be invited to come into yours.

Danny and I invited Jesus to come to our wedding from the first moment we were engaged. In fact, inscribed inside each of our wedding bands is a triangle that signifies there are three of us in this relationship. God is at the apex, Danny and I at the lower corners. Our commitment was that as we grew closer to God individually, we would also draw closer to each other. If you need a miracle in your marriage, start by inviting Jesus into the relationship. You will be blessed, not only by your increased awareness of His Presence, but also by the knowledge that He is there when unexpected problems and crises arise.

Just Give Me Jesus

THAT'S DISGUSTING!

"You are neither cold nor hot.
I wish you were either one or the other!"

REVELATION. 3:15, NIV

I love hot, black coffee and usually have a cup beside me as I work at my desk. But I will get so engrossed in what I am doing that time will pass more quickly than I realize. Again and again, while concentrating on my work, I will absent-mindedly pick up the cup of coffee only to find it is lukewarm. I am glad I am working in private, because my instinctive reaction is to immediately spit the coffee back into the cup!

What an eternal shame it would be if my life caused the Lord to react in the same disgusted way! Yet indifference to Christ was, and still is, disgusting to the Lord! It is incomprehensible to glimpse the glory of Jesus—

The Lord of glory . . .
The Rose of Sharon . . .
The bright Morning Star . . .
and simply shrug! That's disgusting!

What will you do, instead, to live a life that delights Him?

The Vision of His Glory

DOING THINGS GOD'S WAY

"He who abides in Me, and I in him,
bears much fruit; for without Me you can do nothing."

JOHN 15:5, NKJV

After following Jesus' instructions to throw their nets on the other side of the boat, the disciples hauled in a huge catch of fish. Back on the beach, He invited them to "come and have breakfast" (John 21:12, NIV). With furtive glances and downcast faces, "none of the disciples dared ask him, 'Who are you?'" (John 21:12, NIV). They knew. And on that early spring morning beside the sparkling sea, Jesus took the bread and fish from the fire and fed His disciples breakfast! They feasted and were satisfied.

Jesus was teaching them an important life lesson. They had been out in the boat, apparently trying to meet their own needs, doing what they were naturally good at, but basically living their lives without Him. And they had come up empty. Unfulfilled. But when He was in their lives, and they obeyed His Word, and they served Him in His way, not only were they successful, but they were also satisfied!

Just Give Me Jesus

THE PATTERN FOR DISCIPLINE

A faithful man will abound with blessings.

PROVERBS 28:20, NKJV

Our society is increasingly becoming undisciplined. We work if we want to, show up on time if we can make it, and see a job through to the finish if we feel like it, all the while complaining about the pay or seeking more lucrative benefits. God worked persistently and consistently every day, all day long, until the job of creating everything was finished. God understands what it's like to begin each day in the morning, go to work, apply yourself to the project at hand, accomplish a portion of the goal day after day until you complete the job satisfactorily. God's weekly work was timely, orderly, precise, neat, thorough, planned, and goal-oriented.

How closely does the way you do your weekly work reflect His?

God's Story

OUR HEAVENLY HOME

"If I go and prepare a place for you,
I will come again and receive you to Myself;
that where I am there you may be also."

JOHN 14:3, NKJV

Genesis gives us an unforgettable picture of
the Lord God. After at least five "days" of intensely
creative work, He "planted a garden in the east, in
Eden; and there he put the man he had formed.
And the LORD God made all kinds of trees grow out
of the ground—trees that were pleasing to the eye"
(Gen. 2:8–9, NIV). In my mind's eye, I can see Him
on His hands and knees, grubbing in the dirt,
planting trees and flowers, watering and pruning and
landscaping. God Himself was the first homemaker.
We can only imagine the joyful eagerness as He
presented Adam with his lovingly prepared home
that was not just adequate but extravagant.

But the preparations made for that first earthly
home . . . are nothing compared with the
preparations being made for our heavenly home!

Heaven: My Father's House

TRUST HIM!

Commit your way to the LORD,
trust also in Him, and He shall bring it to pass.

PSALM 37:5, NKJV

———

At times our understanding is limited. We simply have to trust our heavenly Father to know best. We have to trust God's silences and respect God's mysteries and wait for God's answers.

When we pray for the healing of a loved one, and he dies . . .

When we pray for release from a financial burden, and we go bankrupt . . .

When we pray for reconciliation, and we are handed divorce papers . . .

When we pray for our career, and we get laid off . . .

When we pray for protection, and we are robbed . . .

We just have to trust Him. Trust Him. *Trust Him!*

My Heart's Cry

RISK-TAKING OBEDIENCE

We ought to obey God rather than men.

ACTS 5:29, NKJV

At the wedding in Cana, Jesus issued a command to the servants that seemed to have nothing to do with the shortage of wine: "Fill the jars with water" (John 2:7, NIV). The servants must have stolen furtive looks at each other, but without question, resistance, or argument, "they filled them to the brim" (John 2:7, NIV).

Why did the servants obey? What made them risk their reputations and their jobs and carry out His instructions? Surely it wasn't just because Mary told them to do whatever He said. It must have been something about Jesus Himself that thrust them out on the limb of risk-taking obedience.

Was it His clear, firm gaze of authority?

Was it the quiet confidence of His demeanor?

Was it the unwavering strength of His tone of voice?

Whatever the reason, they obeyed and experienced the thrill of seeing the water they poured into the jars, pour out as wine!

Just Give Me Jesus

JUNE 19

CONSIDER THE CONSEQUENCES

Do not be deceived, God is not mocked;
for whatever a man sows, that he will also reap.

GALATIANS 6:7, NKJV

Satan never mentions the consequences of sin. He never mentions the psychological trauma that follows an abortion. He never mentions the panic and fear that grip you every time you answer the phone after cheating on your tax return. There are serious consequences to sin. Always. Without exception. Adam ate the forbidden fruit his wife had offered, "Then the eyes of both of them were opened, and they realized they were naked" (Gen. 3:7, NIV).

Satan had told Eve her eyes would be opened and she would be like God, knowing good and evil. Eve's eyes were opened, but in a grotesque way. She knew good, but also that she was separated from it. She knew evil because now she was saturated in it. She knew good and evil in a way God never intended her to know—and she was deeply ashamed.

Before you consciously choose to sin, consider the consequences.

God's Story

RELYING ON GOD ALONE

When the people heard the sound of the trumpet,
and the people shouted with a great shout, . . .
the wall fell down flat.

JOSHUA 6:20, NKJV

God surely gave Joshua the strangest strategy for overcoming Jericho that any general has ever been given! God told him to lead his armed men in a silent march around the outside walls of the city once a day for six days. On the seventh day, they were to march around the city seven times. On the last lap, the priests in the army were to blow trumpets loudly and the people were to shout. Then the wall would collapse, and Joshua's army could successfully capture the city!

God answers prayer, but sometimes the way He goes about it can be incredibly confusing and unconventional, which is one reason He goes about it in that way—so that our faith rests totally in Him. Then, when the answer comes, we know without a shred of doubt that it comes from Him alone and that He knows best. And we give Him all the glory!

Why?

GOD'S SEAL

If anyone does not have the Spirit of Christ,
he is not His.

ROMANS 8:9, NKJV

In the Tabernacle, God had dwelt *among* men.

In the history of Israel, God had spoken *through* man.

In the Gospels, God was visible *as* Man.

But at Pentecost, God became available to dwell in man!

Until that Pentecost two thousand years ago, people were saved by faith in Jesus Christ, even though they didn't know His Name. Their faith was demonstrated by the obedient sacrifices they made at the temple as they symbolically looked forward to the cross. Since Pentecost, we are still saved by faith in Jesus Christ. But our faith looks back to His sacrifice, which has already been made on our behalf at the cross. Additionally, we now have the experience of the indwelling of the Holy Spirit Who seals our "rebirth," or "conversion." Do you bear God's "Seal" of authentic conversion?

Just Give Me Jesus

WASHED IN THE BLOOD

To Him who loved us and washed us
from our sins in His own blood, . . . be glory
and dominion forever and ever.

REVELATION 1:5-6, NKJV

In our pleasure-seeking, anything-goes, feel-good society, guilt is anathema. We run from it through frantic activity, drown it in alcohol, drug it with Prozac, escape it through entertainment, talk about it to a therapist, blame it on someone else, suppress it through mental gymnastics, but we can't rid ourselves of it! It's like a stain that won't come out of our clothes no matter how many wash cycles we put it through or what kind of detergent we use because the stain has become part of the fabric! The only thing that can "wash away" our sin and guilt before God is the blood of Jesus Christ. So God has given us a conscience with a guilt alarm that goes off when sin enters so that we might go to Jesus Christ for cleansing.

God's Story

THE MIGHTY NAME OF JESUS

"I will do whatever you ask in my name,
so that the Son may bring glory to the Father."

JOHN 14:13, NIV

Jesus' name has meaning that reveals Who He is. His name is Lord, which means Jehovah God. He reveals God to you and me. His name is also Jesus, which means Savior, because He came to save us from the penalty of our sin. And His name is Christ, which is the New Testament equivalent of the Old Testament name Messiah. He fulfills all prophecy about the Anointed One of God Who would come to reign and rule on earth.

To pray in Jesus' name means we come to God believing that Jesus is our Lord—believing He has revealed God to us and in response we have submitted to His authority. To pray in Jesus' name means we believe He is our only Savior Whose death on the cross provides atonement for our sin. And it means we acknowledge that He is the Christ, Who is coming again to rule the world in peace and righteousness. Do you believe on the Lord Jesus Christ?

My Heart's Cry

JUNE 24

PASS IT ON

You are a chosen generation, . . . that you may
proclaim the praises of Him who called you out of
darkness into His marvelous light.

1 PETER 2:9, NKJV

"By faith Abel offered a better sacrifice than Cain did. . . . And by faith he still speaks, even though he is dead" (Heb. 11:4, NIV). Abel's life, although brief, was not wasted because of his faith in God, expressed through his witness.

Have you ever wondered what people will think of you when you are gone? What will your grandchildren know about you? Wouldn't it be wonderful, if, like Abel, you are remembered throughout all the generations to follow as one who lived by faith in God?

Like a relay race, Abel passed the baton of truth that leads to faith to the next generation, which was represented by his little brother, Seth. If you are single or childless, you are not exempt from the privilege as well as the responsibility of relaying the baton. While unable to relay it to your own children, you can relay it to someone else's. The possibilities are limitless. So . . . pass it on!

God's Story

THE CHOICE TO REJOICE

Rejoice in the Lord always.
I will say it again: Rejoice!
PHILIPPIANS 4:4, NIV

The apostle Paul knew the secret of victory when he and Silas were thrown into the inner cell of a prison, their feet fastened in stocks, because they had preached the Gospel of Jesus Christ. "About midnight Paul and Silas were praying and singing hymns to God" (Acts 16:24–25, NIV). As a result of their praise, an earthquake collapsed the prison, the jailor was converted, and they were set free! Paul maintained that spirit of praise until the end of his life when he once again found himself in chains in a Roman prison yet emphatically declared, "I will continue to rejoice" (Phil 1:18, NIV).

I doubt if, during either of those imprisonments, Paul felt like praising. But he had learned to walk by faith, not by his feelings. And today he commands you and me to exercise our will, making the deliberate, conscious choice to "rejoice in the Lord always. I will say it again: Rejoice!"

My Heart's Cry

JUNE 26

THE GOD OF ALL COMFORT

Blessed be the God and Father of our
Lord Jesus Christ . . . who comforts us in
all our tribulation.

2 CORINTHIANS 1:3-4, NKJV

Medical studies have proven that worry attacks the central nervous system, the circulatory system, and the digestive system of our bodies.

Noah was exposed to such frightening experiences he could have worried himself to death; after all, he survived the equivalent of a nuclear holocaust. While Sunday school stories conjure up in our minds the picture of Noah as a quaint, folksy, old zookeeper with a plump, rosy-cheeked wife, he was in fact a very strong, courageous man of character and faith who could have been tremendously traumatized by the most violent catastrophe in history.

Surely Noah knew the paralysis of fear and the total paranoia of worry. But he also knew by experience that the God of the storm is also the God of all comfort, able to calm his fears as he kept his faith in God and his focus on God.

God's Story

ATTRACTED TO WEAKNESS

It is because of him that you are in Christ Jesus,
who has become for us wisdom from God.

1 CORINTHIANS 1:30, NIV

Who do you say you can't witness to because he or she is an intellectual, or highly educated, and you are not? Or maybe the person has a seminary degree and you have just started going to church. Remember, it was Joseph, a Hebrew teenager and slave, not the wise men of Egypt, who interpreted Pharaoh's dreams. It was another Hebrew slave, Daniel, not the wise men of Babylon, who deciphered the mysterious writing on the wall of Belshazzar's palace. It was the unlettered fishermen, not the Scribes and the Pharisees, who were taken into the confidence of Christ and used of God to build His church.

Do you feel inadequate intellectually, educationally, socially, theologically? Good! God can use you! He states clearly that He "chose the foolish things of the world to shame the wise" (1 Cor. 1:27, NIV). God is attracted to your weakness!

Just Give Me Jesus

THE DESTRUCTIVENESS OF SIN

Beloved, if God so loved us,
we also ought to love one another.

1 JOHN 4:11, NKJV

The longing of God's heart, if it can be expressed as such, is to be known, loved, glorified, and enjoyed by His creation. Although in His plural nature God has ultimate fellowship, love, and harmony within the Trinity, He also desired fellowship and friendship with Adam and Eve.

But early in their lives Adam and Eve made one choice that broke their relationship with God and cost them their happiness at the present and their destiny for the future, devastating their family for every generation to come. This devastation was inevitable because life is made up of relationships with God, with others, and with ourselves, and the choice to sin through disobedience destroyed all three relationships. Sin destroys our relationship with God through guiltiness. It destroys our relationship with others through lovelessness. It destroys our relationship with ourselves through meaninglessness. What sin is worth such destructive consequences?

God's Story

DO YOU BELIEVE THIS?

"I am the resurrection and the life.
He who believes in me will live, even though he dies."

JOHN 11:25, NIV

Do *you* believe this? Do you believe that . . .
when there is no hope,
when there is no recourse,
when there is no answer,
when there is no help,
when there is no way,
when there is no remedy,
when there is no solution,
when there is nobody,
there *is hope* if you have Jesus?! Do you believe that
Jesus can make a way when there is no way?
With Jesus, all things are possible!

Why?

CREATED EQUAL

*As we have opportunity, let us do good to all,
especially to those who are of the household of faith.*

GALATIANS 6:10, NKJV

When God "breathed into his nostrils the breath of life, and the man became a living being" (Gen. 2:7, NIV), all human life became sacred because it came directly from God. Whether a person is a murderer on death row or the most beloved person in town, each one is to be treated with respect if for no other reason than human life comes from God.

Are you prejudiced toward someone? A person of a different race or educational background or economic level? Someone from another culture or denomination or religion? Someone with a different language or social status or skin color? There is absolutely no room for prejudice of any kind in a life that follows the Creator's directions. All men are created equal, not in abilities or opportunities, but in the eyes of God because all men derive their lives from God.

God's Story

July

You are in God's heart and on His mind every moment.

GOD'S WAY HOME

"I am the way and the truth and the life.
No one comes to the Father except through me."

JOHN 14:6, NIV

Jesus did not say that He knew the way to heaven; He said that He Himself is the only Way to get there!

During the Vietnam War, a story was reported about a paratrooper who had been air-dropped into the jungle and couldn't find his way out. A native guide had to be sent into the jungle to find the lost man then lead him safely to his base. The guide became the man's way to safety—his "way home." In the same manner, Jesus is "God's Guide," heaven-dropped into the world to lead lost sinners safely "Home." It stands to reason that if you refuse to acknowledge that you are "lost," then you will not accept God's Way home. But for those of us who know we have been lost, our overwhelming gratitude for the Guide is enough to compel us to tell others about Him—about the truth of their lost condition and the truth about the Way out.

My Heart's Cry

THE KEEPER

*The Son is the radiance of God's glory and
the exact representation of his being,
sustaining all things by his powerful word.*

HEBREWS 1:3, NIV

With His unlimited power, the Living Logos of God not only created all things but even today He still sustains "all things by his powerful word." Who do you know who says he doesn't need God? Think about it for a moment!

Our planet is ninety-three million miles away from the sun. If the sun were any closer to earth, we would burn up. If it were any farther away from earth, we would freeze.

Our planet tilts exactly 23 degrees on its axis, giving us four seasons a year. If it tilted at any other angle, we would have massive continents of ice.

And Who keeps all this in perfect order? Who keeps planets from spinning out of control, or stars from falling from the sky? The answer is none other than the Living Logos of Almighty God. If He can keep the universe in order, He can keep your life and mine in order, too.

Just Give Me Jesus

POWER TO OVERCOME

*This is the victory that has
overcome the world, even our faith.*

1 JOHN 5:4, NIV

Praise God for the glorious dawn of His story! He is separate from and greater than Creation, yet He chose to humble Himself and become part of it when He took on the form of a man. And as Man, the One Who is greater than Creation submitted Himself to it—to the heat of the day, the cold of the night, the storms on the sea. On occasion, His deity was revealed when He calmed the sea or cleansed the leper or gave sight to the blind or raised the dead, but for the most part of thirty-three years, He lived in subjection to the very things He had created. Why? So that you and I might have the power, through faith in Him, to overcome the empty, broken, sinful, bitter, meaningless, lonely, helpless, fearful, weak, religious, and hopeless world of which we are a part.

God's Story

FREE AT LAST!

Being found in appearance as a man, he humbled himself and became obedient to death—even death on a cross!

PHILIPPIANS 2:8, NIV

How awesome to consider that the Creator of the universe, unbound in time and space for all eternity, chose to be bound

by a woman's womb for nine months,

by the body of a man that knew weariness and hunger,

by a Roman cross, with His hands and feet pinned by spikes,

by a borrowed tomb . . .

Why? So that you and I might be set free from the problems that threaten to bind us and keep us from fulfilling God's intended purpose for our lives.

Praise God! We can be free, truly free at last, from all that binds us, because the One Who is gloriously eternal, unbound by time and space, was willing to be bound!

God's Story

JUST TURN ON THE LIGHT!

*You were once darkness, but now you are light
in the Lord. Walk as children of light.*

EPHESIANS 5:8, NKJV

I live in the southern part of the United States. During the warmer months in particular, if I leave the porch light on at night, all sorts of moths and insects swarm to it. The variety can be fascinating. Everything from large luna moths to beetles to strange green crawly things beat and flutter their way to the light. I have never stood at the door and called these insects to come or set out bait for them. All I have to do is to turn on the light and they come of their own volition—by the hundreds. Moths, in the midst of the darkness, are not attracted to more darkness. They are attracted to the light.

People today, living in the midst of "darkness," are not attracted to more darkness; they are attracted to the Light. So let your Light shine! Lift it high! You don't have to have a clever presentation to your witness or learn evangelistic formulas or take a course on communicating to postmodern man. For heaven's sake, *just turn on the Light!*

Just Give Me Jesus

A FOOT BATH

"A person who has had a bath needs only to wash his feet; his whole body is clean. And you are clean. . . ."

JOHN 13:10, NIV

In Jesus' day the people went to common baths, similar to a public swimming pool, where they would bathe all over. However, as soon as they left the bath and walked along the streets, their feet would get dirty again. So when they arrived at their homes, it was not necessary to have a complete bath. They only needed to wash their feet of the dust and dirt they had picked up along the way.

Jesus was explaining to Peter that once you and I have been to the cross for our complete "bath," we are clean. All of our sin—past, present, future, small, medium, large—is washed away by the blood of Jesus and we are totally, completely, permanently forgiven! Praise God! But we still sin! Our feet get dirty again! So every day we come back to the cross, not for forgiveness since we are already forgiven, but to confess our sin and be cleansed that we might maintain a right fellowship with God and with others and ourselves. Do you need a foot bath?

My Heart's Cry

THE LIGHT OF THE WORLD

*"The light has come into the world,
and men loved darkness rather than light.,
because their deeds were evil."*

JOHN 3:19. NKJV

Jesus Christ is the true Light that gives light to every man and woman. There is no other light! Other religions and peoples may have some truth, but only Jesus Christ is *the* truth for everyone who has ever been born into the human race, regardless of culture, age, nationality, generation, heritage, gender, color, or language.

There is not a Light for America and a Light for Africa and a Light for China and a Light for Europe and a Light for India—there is only one Light for the entire world for all time, for every person, and His name is Jesus. That's why John bore witness to the Light. That's why you and I share our faith, present the Gospel, and refuse to be intimidated by a multicultural, pluralistic world.

Just Give Me Jesus

THE BLIGHT OF SIN

*"You are already clean because
of the word I have spoken to you."*

JOHN 15:3, NIV

There is one primary "internal blight" that attacks the branches of the Vine, which, if not severely dealt with, will destroy our fruitfulness. The "blight" is sin. Sin obstructs the free flow of the "sap" of the Holy Spirit in our lives. And since the Holy Spirit is the One Who truly produces the fruit that we bear, anything that grieves or quenches Him affects our fruitfulness. Jesus addressed the necessity of confronting sin in our lives when He confirmed, "You are already clean because of the word I have spoken to you." The disciples were already clean because they had placed their faith in Him and given Him their hearts. They continued to be cleansed as they listened to His Word and applied and obeyed it.

In the same way, you and I are clean when we place our faith in Jesus Christ as our Savior, then give Him our hearts in total surrender. We continue to be cleansed as every day we live by His Word, which we read, apply, and obey. How free-flowing is the "Sap" in your life?

My Heart's Cry

YOUR ULTIMATE GOOD

In all things God works for the good of those who
love him, who have been called according to his purpose.
ROMANS 8:28, NIV

Romans 8:28 says, "in all things God works for the good of those who love him, who have been called according to his purpose." In other words, when you are in the purpose, or will, of God, everything that comes into your life can work for your good. You may immediately question how the pregnancy of your unmarried daughter can work for your good, or how God can work even a divorce for your good, or how the loss of your job can be for your good, or how your terminal illness can be for your good. If, by "good," Romans 8:28 meant your comfort, convenience, health, wealth, prosperity, pleasure, or happiness, we would all question it! But your ultimate good is conformity to the image of Jesus Christ. And when you are in God's will— "called according to his purpose"—everything God allows into your life is used by Him to make you like Christ. *Everything!*

The Vision of His Glory

JULY 10

WAIT . . .

Those who wait on the LORD shall renew their strength;
they shall mount up with wings like eagles.

ISAIAH 30:31, NKJV

Joshua had to wait seven days as he obediently marched around Jericho before God rewarded his patience and brought the walls down.

Israel waited for the Messiah to come. Mary waited nine months for Jesus' birth. Jesus waited for the woman of Samaria to come to the well, Mary and Martha waited for Jesus to come to Bethany, and Jesus Himself waited three days in the tomb for the resurrection. A person who lives in submissive obedience to Christ is a person who is often called to wait.

Are you waiting on God for something? What plans have you made in the meantime? Who else have you involved in those plans? Is there someone else, a mother-in-law or pastor or best friend, who is leading you to join him or her in decisive action? Instead of blindly saying, "I'll go with you," take a moment to pray and ask God for His direction. Then wait until He answers you.

Just Give Me Jesus

JULY 11

A VESSEL OF BEAUTY

Like clay in the hand of the potter, so are you in my hand.

JEREMIAH 18:6, NIV

The old clay pot was cracked, shattered, and broken. So the man took it to the Potter, Who broke it down even further, moistening the clay with water, making it soft and pliable before He put it on His wheel. Then He began to remake it into a vessel pleasing to Himself. He firmly applied pressure on some areas, touched lightly on other areas, added more clay to a specific spot that needed filling, and removed clay that hindered and marred the shape He had in mind. As He turned the wheel, His loving, gentle hands never left the clay as He molded and made it after His will.

Finally, the Potter was finished. He took what had once been a broken clay pot off the wheel, but now it was unrecognizable. It had been transformed into a vessel of beauty. The Potter put it in His showcase that others might see the revelation of His glory in the work that He does.

God is the Potter. You are His clay. How pliable are you to the soft, firm pressure of His touch?

God's Story

FACING THE FUTURE WITH HOPE

Then I, John, saw the holy city, New Jerusalem,
coming down out of heaven from God.
REVELATION 21:2, NKJV

Exiled to the island of Patmos in the midst of the Aegean Sea, the apostle John knew he would be facing death in the not-too-distant future. This was the very moment in time when God chose to give John a vision of the glory of Jesus Christ! This vision included a tantalizing glimpse into Heaven, where one day God Himself will live forever with His people. This glorious vision has been recorded in the final book of the Bible, Revelation, because John was commanded to write down what he saw. The vision was to be not only for his own personal comfort and encouragement but for all people down through the centuries who, when facing daily challenges, extraordinary circumstances, or even when plunging to certain death, could do so with courage and *with hope*.

Heaven: My Father's House

JESUS WEEPS WITH YOU

In all their affliction He was afflicted; . . .
in His love and in His pity He redeemed them.

ISAIAH 63:9, NKJV

When was the last time you wept into your pillow at night, thinking no one cared? Is the pain so deep and your hurt so great that you cry night after night? In your misery and loneliness, do you think Jesus is emotionally detached? That He just doesn't care? Or that He's simply too busy to notice? Or that He is somewhat callous since He sees a lot of pain that's worse than yours? Or that *He* couldn't possibly understand how *you feel?* Or that *He's not concerned enough* to meet your needs?

Did you know that *Jesus weeps with you?* Did you know He puts all your tears in a bottle because they are precious to Him? (Ps. 56:8, NKJV) He has said in all of your afflictions, He Himself is afflicted. Why? Because He understands! And *He loves you!*

Your suffering is His.

Your grief is His.

Your tears are on His face!

Why?

SEPARATE FROM THE WORLD

"You do not belong to the world, but I have chosen you out of the world. That is why the world hates you."

JOHN 15:19, NIV

Separation from the world is logical, since we operate on a totally different level in every area of our lives. But separation is also a command we are to obey for our own benefit, lest we be pressed into the world's mold. However, separation from the world requires a certain amount of courage, because the world often views our separation as an indictment of itself and resents us for it.

Jesus underscored our separation from the world when He said, "You do not belong to the world, but I have chosen you out of the world. That is why the world hates you."

Hates you? Do you doubt this? Then I suggest you take a strong public stand for the uniqueness of Who Jesus is, for the truth of the Bible from cover to cover, for the necessity of living a life of integrity. Then count the seconds before someone labels you an extreme fanatical element of the religious right! But while the world may mock you, heaven applauds you!

My Heart's Cry

FULFILLING THE LAW

The law was our tutor to bring us to Christ,
that we might be justified by faith.

GALATIANS 3:24, NKJV

Think of the law as summed up in the Ten Commandments.

The law didn't make us feel better. It made us feel worse.

The law didn't help us to be good. It revealed how bad we were.

The law didn't give us joy or peace. It made us feel guilty.

The law didn't help us measure up. It showed us we fall short.

The apostle Paul said the law was like our schoolmaster, teaching us how much we need a Savior. But "grace and truth came through Jesus Christ" (John 1:17b, NIV) because He perfectly fulfills the law. His life measures up to the standard established by the law, and when we receive Him by faith, His righteousness is credited to us. Therefore *in Christ* we too fulfill the law.

Just Give Me Jesus

THE THREAT TO OUR ENVIRONMENT

We know that the whole creation has been groaning
as in the pains of childbirth right up to the present time.
ROMANS 8:22, NIV

God created you and me to live with Him in His heavenly home, enjoying fellowship with Him and glorifying Him forever! Death was not part of His plan. It was through Adam's sin that death—temporal and eternal—entered the human race. And death entered creation as well.

Flowers fade. Grass withers. Birds sing in minor key. Trees lose their leaves because "creation was subjected to frustration, not by its own choice, but by the will of the one who subjected it, in hope that the creation itself will be liberated from its bondage to decay and brought into the glorious freedom of the children of God" (Rom. 8:20–21, NIV). Because of man's sin, creation has been in a cycle of death and decay. The greatest threat to our environment is not fluorocarbon or nuclear testing or the burning of tropical forests in the Amazon River region or toxic waste. The greatest threat to our environment has been and is sin! So . . . help to clean up the environment by repenting of your sin!

God's Story

GOD'S GREATER PURPOSE

*"This sickness will not end in death. No, it is for
God's glory so that God's Son may be glorified through it."*

JOHN 11:4, NIV

Why does God let things go from bad to worse for those He loves—those like *me?* Like Martha and Mary?

Yet, consider this: When Jesus expressed words of encouragement concerning Lazarus' condition, Lazarus had already died! (John 11:4) Was Jesus *lying?* Was His promise some sort of empty *"hope so"?* Was He just *toying* with Martha and Mary's feelings? NO! What Jesus said meant . . .

that Lazarus' sickness did not have physical death as its ultimate purpose.

that God has a greater purpose than our immediate comfort.

that getting what we want, when we want it, is not always the best for us or glorifying to God.

Would you tell God now, in prayer, that you want what He wants more than what you want? Then trust Him!

Why?

OPEN YOUR EYES TO JESUS

"He will bring glory to me by taking from
what is mine and making it known to you."

JOHN 16:14, NIV

The world sees Jesus as a man, perhaps even a good or great man and possibly even a prophet, but still a man. It is the Holy Spirit Who opens our spiritual eyes of understanding so that we see Jesus as much more than just a man. We see Him as: our Creator-the Jehovah of the Old Testament-the long-awaited Messiah-the only Son of God-the Savior of the world-the Good Shepherd-the risen Lord-the Judge of the universe-the reigning and ruling King of kings!

The only way we can be convinced of Who Jesus is, is through the enlightenment we have received from the Holy Spirit. Jesus explained, "When he, the Spirit of truth, comes, he will guide you into all truth. . . . He will bring glory to me by taking from what is mine and making it known to you" (John 16:13–14, NIV). So . . . the next time you read your Bible, pray first and ask the Spirit of Truth to open your eyes to Jesus.

Just Give Me Jesus

THE RIGHTEOUS REMNANT

*The righteousness of the blameless
will direct his way aright.*
PROVERBS 11:5, NKJV

Just as certain physical characteristics are passed from one generation to another, so truth that leads to faith in God is passed from one generation to another. This is subtly revealed by the fact that Adam's life is not recorded in the genealogy of his firstborn, Cain, but in the genealogy of his third son, Seth. (Gen. 5:5–31) It was Seth's descendants who relayed faith in God while Cain's descendants rebelled against Him and therefore wasted their lives.

Age is not mentioned in the list of Cain's descendants while in Adam's genealogy the years of each man's life are carefully recorded. God lovingly counts the years of those in the righteous remnant, because they glorify Him.

Are you a spiritual descendent of Adam as well as a physical descendant? If the Lamb's book of life were opened today, would your name be found there? If you have been validated as an authentic child of God, your life has eternal meaning and priceless value in His sight.

God's Story

SPENDING TIME WITH GOD

O God, You are my God;
early will I seek You; my soul thirsts for You.

PSALM 63:1, NKJV

God seemed to come to my door one day and ask if I would start walking with Him by getting up early in the morning for prayer and Bible reading. At first I thought it was something I *had* to do. I dragged my feet because I found I didn't want to sacrifice the extra few minutes of sleep! He was so patient as He waited for me to understand that it wasn't something I had to do; instead it was a personal time of fellowship where I could just grow in my love relationship with Him.

One reason I have maintained my walk with God is that no one else, not my beloved husband and children or my precious mother and father or my close and loyal friends, really understands me. No one else truly knows my fears and longings and hurts and dreams and failures. But He shares my feelings, my loneliness. Spending time with God as I "walk" with Him meets needs that are in the deepest part of me. He Himself is the solution to the loneliness of the human spirit.

God's Story

JULY 21

THE HOLY SPIRIT CHANGES MINDS

"When he [the Holy Spirit] comes, he will convict the world of guilt in regard to sin and righteousness."

JOHN 16:8, NIV

Jesus Christ was crucified as a criminal, as a blaspheming heretic, as an enemy of Rome and of God. What changed the world's opinion of Him? Why does He go down in history as a good Man? Why do people put their trust in a crucified Jew two thousand years after He lived on earth? The change in opinion was brought about by none other than the Holy Spirit Who convinced the world of the truth—that Jesus Christ was not only crucified, but that He rose from the dead! He's alive! Jesus announced to His disciples that "when he [the Holy Spirit] comes, he will convict the world of guilt . . . in regard to righteousness" (John 16:8–10, NIV). The proof of the righteousness of Jesus Christ is in the fact that God didn't leave Him on the cross, bearing your sin and mine, but raised Him from the dead and seated Him at His right hand, placing all authority in the universe under His feet!

Who do you know who needs to change his mind about Jesus? Pray for that person.

My Heart's Cry

GOD'S BOUNDARIES

"You are free to eat from any tree in the garden;
but You must not eat from the tree
of the knowledge of good and evil. . . ."

GENESIS 2:17, NIV

———

In the first home, the Lord God taught man the difference between right and wrong. Adam needed to know what his boundaries were, what was acceptable to God and what was not.

Can you imagine the chaos that would result if a multilane highway had no painted markings to give direction to the traffic? Accidents and confusion would be the order of the day. No one complains about the markings because drivers know they exist for their own safety.

Today we are surrounded by a generation of people who have grown up living according to their own moral codes, defying the boundaries set by God. As a result, it is a generation with no peace or sense of security. The statistics on crime, divorce, abortion, and suicide give eloquent witness to the danger of living outside God's boundaries. He has drawn the lines—we need to stay within them!

God's Story

PRAYING IN FAITH

Without faith it is impossible to please God,
because anyone who comes to him must believe that he
exists and that he rewards those who earnestly seek him.

HEBREWS 11:6, NIV

Have you based your faith . . .

on what someone else has told you God wants to do for you?

on what you have seen Him do for another person?

on what you think is fair or loving?

on what you think would be in the best interest of those involved?

on a doctor's recommendation for treatment?

You and I must pray in faith, or our prayer will not be pleasing to God. If your faith as you pray is based on *anything other* than faith in God's specific promise given to you in His Word, then your prayer is on a shaky foundation. So ask God to give you a promise from His Word on which you can pray in faith.

Why?

EXTRAVAGANT THANKS

Then Noah built an altar to the LORD and,
. . . he sacrificed burnt offerings on it.

GENESIS 8:20, NIV

Noah took one-seventh of all of his flocks and herds and offered them in an extravagant sacrifice to the God of his salvation! Surely the sacrifice was one

of praise to God for His faithfulness and greatness,

of thanksgiving to God for His grace to save himself and his family,

of repentance from anything that would not be pleasing to God,

of rededication of his life to the One Who had saved it.

Noah must have been totally overwhelmed by the awareness that out of all the people who had been living on Planet Earth, God had saved him. Why? It was just God's grace! His heart must have felt ready to burst with the intensity of his gratitude. There could be no other way to express what was in his heart than to give back to God the life that He alone had saved. How can you and I do less?

God's Story

THE SAP OF HIS SPIRIT

"As the branch cannot bear fruit of itself, unless it abides
in the vine, neither can you, unless you abide in Me."

JOHN 15:4, NKJV

⸎ The branches of a vine "abide" by just remaining connected to the vine. Permanently. Consistently. Day after day, week after week, year after year. They simply rest in their position, allowing the sap of the vine to flow freely through them. They exert no effort of their own. The fruit that is subsequently borne on the branch is actually produced by the life-giving sap within.

To abide in Christ means to remain connected to Him so completely that the "sap" of His Spirit flows through every part of your being, including your mind, will, and emotions as well as your words and deeds. The "fruit" that you then bear is actually produced by His Spirit in you through no conscious effort of your own. If you and I want to be fruitful, we do not concentrate on fruit-bearing; we concentrate on our personal relationship with Jesus Christ.

My Heart's Cry

ETERNALLY BLESSED

By faith Abraham, when called to go to a place he
would later receive as his inheritance, obeyed and went.

HEBREWS 11:8, NIV

⟡ It was as though Abraham had been waiting
all his life for the call from God, and when he
received it, he responded immediately with steadfast
faith, and hope.

Through Abraham, God began the long process
of accomplishing His plan to provide the Redeemer.
Abraham's family became the chosen nation of Israel
that provided the audiovisual aid of the sacrifices and
ceremonies that pictured for the world God's terms
for man to have a right relationship with Himself. It
was also Abraham's descendants who recorded the
revelation of God through the written prophecy,
history, biography, and poetry that we call the Bible.
And it was Abraham's descendants who provided the
human lineage for Jesus Christ.

I'm so grateful Abraham answered God's call!
My life is eternally blessed. I wonder . . . who will
be blessed because I have answered God's call?

God's Story

TRIUMPH OVER SUFFERING

In the time of trouble He shall hide me in His pavilion;
in the secret place of His tabernacle He shall hide me.
PSALM 27:5, NKJV

Believers of every generation have triumphed over their suffering as they placed their faith in God, trusting Him even when they didn't understand why. And every generation *has* suffered to a greater or lesser degree.

My generation has not been exempt. There has been unfathomable hopelessness and helplessness in the killing fields of Cambodia under the Khmer Rouge, in the massacres under the vicious anarchy of the Red Guard in China, in the senseless slaughter between tribes in Rwanda, in the torture chambers supervised by the butcher of Baghdad. . . . Sometimes it's just so hard to understand!

Yet God is bigger than our suffering. We can have hope as we place our trust in Him—in His faithfulness and in His ability to work out in our lives His purposes that will be for our ultimate good and His eternal glory. So . . . when you suffer, just trust Him!

Why?

THE DESIRES OF YOUR HEART

Delight yourself in the Lord and he will give you
the desires of your heart. Commit your way to the Lord;
trust in him and he will do this.

PSALM 37:4–5, NIV

In the beginning, Adam was single. Increasingly he longed for a companion with whom he could share his life. He didn't have to beg God or beat the bushes or spend every Saturday night in a singles bar. He just went to sleep in God's will. I wonder if, as he drifted off to sleep, he was praying that God would somehow take away the strange ache in his heart and the loneliness he felt inside, especially when he had observed that every animal had a partner except himself. "So the LORD God caused the man to fall into a deep sleep; and while he was sleeping, he took one of the man's ribs and closed up the place with flesh. Then the LORD God made a woman from the rib he had taken out of the man" (Gen. 2:21–22, NIV). In His wisdom, God knew exactly how to meet Adam's emotional needs—by presenting Adam with a wife. And He knows how to meet your needs and satisfy your desires, too. So . . . commit your way to Him and trust Him!

God's Story

GOD AS MAN

He was in the world, and though the world was made through him, the world did not recognize him.

JOHN 1:10, NIV

If we think we can avoid God by pleading indifference toward Him or ignorance of Him, we're mistaken; both choices are indirect rejection. John makes this point when he states, "He was in the world, and though the world was made through him, the world did not recognize him." It would be easier to imagine Ford Motor Company not recognizing Henry Ford, or Microsoft not recognizing Bill Gates, or the United States of America not recognizing George Washington than to imagine man not recognizing his Creator!

Just about everybody you and I know fails to recognize Jesus for Who He is. The majority of the world doesn't recognize Him for Who He is. The world talks of and teaches evolution as the beginning of all things. The world talks of and teaches about Jesus Christ as a good man or a well-meaning prophet or a revolutionary zealot. But the world does not recognize Jesus Christ for Who He really is: *God as Man!*

Just Give Me Jesus

EVERY KNEE WILL BOW

God also has highly exalted Him and given Him
the name which is above every name,
that at the name of Jesus every knee should bow.
PHILIPPIANS 2:9–10, NKJV

The Bible says that one day, "at the name of Jesus every knee should bow . . . in heaven, and on earth, and under the earth, and that every tongue should confess that Jesus Christ is Lord" (Phil. 2:10–11, NKJV). Whether we want to or not, one day we will *all* bow before God's only Son.

Who do you know who has set him- or herself against Christ?

A school administrator?

A business employer?

A secular corporation?

A religious institution?

A political agenda?

A government policy?

An entire culture?

Whoever, or whatever, sets themselves against Christ will find themselves sooner or later on their faces before Him! So . . . bow down now!

Just Give Me Jesus

ANOTHER COUNSELOR

"I will ask the Father, and he will give you another
Counselor to be with you forever—the Spirit of truth."

JOHN 14:16–17, NIV

Jesus described the Holy Spirit as "Another."
The Greek word actually means "another who is
exactly the same." So although the Holy Spirit is a
distinct person, He is exactly the same as Jesus, but
without the physical body.

We know that Jesus is in heaven. As the first
martyr, Stephen, was being stoned to death, he
looked up and saw heaven open and Jesus standing
at God's right hand, preparing to welcome him
home! (Acts 7:56) But that doesn't mean Jesus has
left us to stumble through the darkness of the future
on our own. He promised His disciples that when
He went to heaven, He would ask His Father to
send down to earth "Another." Jesus called Him the
Counselor (John 14:16), because He is readily
available to give us wisdom for our decisions,
direction for our future, and management for our
responsibilities.

Just Give Me Jesus

August

When I don't understand why,
I trust Him because He loves me.

DETECTING COUNTERFEITS

I will heal them and reveal
to them the abundance of peace and truth.

JEREMIAH 33:6, NKJV

Years ago my mother was invited to a very prestigious dinner party in London, England. As she conversed, Mother discovered that the older gentleman seated beside her was the former head of Scotland Yard. Fascinated, she respectfully began to probe him for anecdotes. As he opened up under her genuine interest, he revealed that the departments under his authority had included those for forgery and counterfeiting. When she surmised that he must have spent a lot of time studying counterfeit signatures, he corrected her. "On the contrary, Mrs. Graham. I spent all of my time studying the genuine thing. That way, when I saw a counterfeit, I could immediately detect it."

My mother's dinner partner had unwittingly touched on a very important principle. If you and I want to be able to detect counterfeit truth, we need to immerse ourselves in the real thing. We need to saturate ourselves in the truth of the Word of God.

Just Give Me Jesus

SEPARATE FROM HIS CREATION

He stirs up the sea with His power,
and by His understanding He breaks up the storm. . . .
Indeed these are the mere edges of His ways.

JOB 26:12, 14, NKJV

God Himself is not *in* a sunset or *in* an act of human compassion any more than an artist is in his painting or a musician is in his music. You and I may see *reflections* of the artist's or musician's personality in his work, but the person himself is separate from it. Likewise, you may see the reflection of God's personality in a sunset or in an act of compassion, but He Himself is not *in* either one. He is separate from His Creation. What an important truth! This means:

When something is wrong, He can right it.
When something is broken, He can mend it.
When something is lost, He can find it.
When something doesn't work, He can fix it.
When something is hurt, He can heal it.

My failures, sins, mistakes, and shortcomings— and yours—in no way dilute or deplete or weaken or harm *God!*

God's Story

THE HOME OF YOUR DREAMS

"I am making everything new!"
REVELATION 21:5, NIV

We all have dreams of what home should be like. . . . Do you dream of a home with love and laughter and loyalty, with family and fun and freedom?

Do you dream of a home where you are accepted, encouraged, and challenged, forgiven, understood, and comforted?

There is hope! The home you've always wanted, the home you continue to long for with all your heart, is the home God is preparing for you! As John gazed at a vision of the glory of Jesus Christ . . . , he stood in awed wonder of "a new heaven and a new earth" (Rev. 21:1, NIV). What he saw was confirmed by the words of One Who was seated on the throne: "I am making everything new!" Imagine it: One day, in the dream home of My Father's House, *everything* will be brand-new and you will live in the home of your dreams!

Heaven: My Father's House

GOD SPEAKS TO US PERSONALLY

"His sheep follow him because they know his voice."

JOHN 10:4, NIV

The Shepherd speaks to us personally—by name. He knows us inside and out. And when He speaks, it's in the language of our own personal lives, through a verse or passage of Scripture that just seems to leap up off the page with our name on it.

Again and again God has seemed to speak to me through the pages of my Bible, giving me the secret to restoring love in my marriage when it had run out, reassuring me of my son's recovery to health before his cancer surgery, directing me again and again in the expansion and priorities in ministry, leading me out of one church and into another. In fact, I do not make a major decision, especially one involving others, without a specific word from my Shepherd.

God speaks personally—are you listening?

My Heart's Cry

THE GREATNESS OF GOD'S POWER

*All things were made through Him, and without Him
nothing was made that was made.*

JOHN 1:3, NKJV

God created:
atoms and angels and ants,
crocodiles and chiggers and clouds,
elephants and eagles and electrons,
orchids and onions and octopuses,
frogs and feathers and sea foam,
diamonds and dust and dinosaurs,
raindrops and sweat drops,
dewdrops and blood drops,
and me! And you!

The greatness of His power to create and design and form and mold and make and build and arrange defies the limits of our imagination. And since He created everything, there is nothing beyond His power to fix or mend or heal or restore!

Just Give Me Jesus

INSTINCTIVE RECOGNITION

The heavens declare the glory of God;
and the firmament shows His handiwork.

PSALM 19:1, NKJV

In his letter to the Romans, the apostle Paul held the entire human race accountable for basic knowledge of God, which he declared "is plain to them, because . . . God's invisible qualities . . . have been clearly seen, being understood from what has been made, so that men are without excuse" (Rom. 1:19–20, NIV). Even tribal people isolated in jungle huts or desert tents have the fundamental testimony of creation. Through the faithfulness of the sun to rise and set, through the miracle of reproduction and birth, and through a myriad of other silent witnesses, the human race has been confronted with the truth.

The real reason many people reject Jesus, at least in the Western Hemisphere, is repression and rejection of what they instinctively know to be the truth—that there is one, true, living God who created us all and has revealed Himself through the Person of Jesus Christ.

Just Give Me Jesus

TRANSFORMED INTO HIS LIKENESS

And we, who with unveiled faces
all reflect the Lord's glory, are being transformed into
his likeness with ever-increasing glory.

2 CORINTHIANS 3:18, NIV

Do you want to experience real, lasting, God-pleasing change so that you are filled with satisfaction, peace, joy, love, purpose—abundant life? Then don't look to a bottle, a pill, a therapist, a once-a-week trip to church. Look to God's Word for yourself. Read your Bible every day in order to understand, apply, and obey it.

As we long to grow not only in our faith but in our Christian character so that others can readily see Christ in us, we need to live in the power of the Holy Spirit and in obedience to His Word. This transformation is a continual process that is brought about by daily saturating ourselves in the Scriptures then living it out on the anvil of our experience, until even our friends exclaim, "I see Jesus in you!"

God's Story

LIVING WITH INCOMPATIBILITY

"As the Father has loved me,
so have I loved you. Now remain in my love."

JOHN 15:9, NIV

Is there someone who comes to your mind as being totally incompatible with you? A parent? Or sibling? Or spouse? Or roommate? Or child? Or supervisor? Or employer?

Have you felt incompatibility was reason enough to sever the relationship? Or at least to avoid it at all costs? Yet there are times when we have no option but to live with or work with or be thrown together with someone who totally contradicts our own personalities and natures. At such times the relationship can become so strained that we can even perceive the incompatible person as an enemy. But there is another way . . .

Jesus focused His disciples on His way of dealing with incompatibility. The key is to make our relationship with Jesus the priority of our lives. Jesus reminded His disciples, "As the Father has loved me, so have I loved you. Now remain in my love."

My Heart's Cry

DISCOVER HIS POWER

I pray . . . that you may know . . .
his incomparably great power for us who believe.

EPHESIANS 1:18–19, NIV

⟋◯ What problem are you facing that is bigger than you are? Praise God for the omnipotence of Jesus Christ! He is the Almighty—mightier than all. Greater, more powerful, than any problem or situation you or I will ever face. In fact, one reason God allows us to have problems and be in situations that seem bigger than we are is so we can discover His "incomparably great power for us who believe."

If our lives are easy, and if all we ever attempt for God is what we know we can handle, how will we ever experience His omnipotence in our lives?

It is when we are in over our heads . . .
when we are cornered with no way out . . .
when we are facing the Red Sea in front of us,
 the desert on either side of us,
  and the Egyptian
   army in back of us . . .
that's when we discover His power!

The Vision of His Glory

TAKE UP YOUR CROSS

*God forbid that I should boast except in the cross
of our Lord Jesus Christ, by whom the world has been
crucified to me, and I to the world.*

GALATIANS 6:14, NKJV

The cross is not just a symbol of love or a fashion statement. The cross is your daily decision to deny yourself . . .

your rights,

your wants,

your dreams,

your plans,

your goals,

and deliberately, wholeheartedly, unreservedly live out your commitment to His will and His way and His Word and His wisdom. The cross is your decision to live for Jesus. Period. No "ifs," "ands," "buts," or "maybes."

Would you take up your cross . . . every day . . . and follow Him?

Just Give Me Jesus

RADICAL LOVE

"Greater love has no one than this,
that one lay down his life for his friends."

JOHN 15:13, NIV

We love others
   who meet our needs,
      whom we get along with,
         who make us feel good.

In essence, our first concern is for our own well-being and having our own needs met, and we love others in proportion to the extent they fulfill those purposes. Our second concern is that others respond positively to our overtures; if they don't, we refuse to continue to love them. But Jesus outlined a radically different kind of love—a love that puts the needs and well-being of others before our own to the extent we would sacrifice our time, our energy, our money, and our thoughts in order to demonstrate it. We are to demonstrate it to others whom we may not like or with whom we may be incompatible or who respond negatively or who may never do anything for us in return! Now that's radical!

My Heart's Cry

OUR ONE FOUNDATION

No one can lay any foundation
other than the one already laid, which is Jesus Christ.

I CORINTHIANS 3:11, NIV

All around us we see lives collapsing with broken hearts and broken homes and broken hopes—with shattered minds and shattered emotions and shattered bodies. What has gone wrong? The foundation on which the majority of people are building their lives is cracked and flawed.

The Bible tells us there is only one foundation for individual or national life that will last, regardless of the crisis or pressure, and it is the foundation of Jesus Christ: "For no one can lay any foundation other than the one already laid, which is Jesus Christ."

Jesus Christ never changes. (Heb. 13:8) He will never leave you nor forsake you. (Heb. 13:5) Nothing can ever separate you from His love. (Rom. 8:35–39) So make sure you are prepared for the storms of life because your life is built on the solid foundation of Jesus Christ.

God's Story

AUGUST 13

TOGETHER FOREVER

We eagerly await a Savior . . . who . . . will transform
our lowly bodies so that they will be like his glorious body.

PHILIPPIANS 3:20-21, NIV

As wonderful as my loved ones are and as much as I miss them, they are not perfect! And if your loved ones are like mine, your relationship with them on earth has not been perfect either. To think of living forever in the same home with my brother would give one pause! But when we get to Heaven, the joy of seeing our loved ones once again is immeasurably increased when we realize that *all* of us will indeed be perfect! There will be no more . . .

disagreements or cross words,

hurt feelings or misunderstandings,

neglect or busyness,

interruptions or rivalry,

jealousy or pride,

selfishness or sin of any kind!

There will be nothing at all to mar our full enjoyment of being with our loved ones forever and ever!

Heaven: My Father's House

GUIDED INTO A DEEPER LEVEL

*"When he, the Spirit of truth, comes,
he will guide you into all truth."*

JOHN 16:13, NIV

⟡ One reason I never approach the Scripture without praying first is because it is the person of the Holy Spirit Who clarifies the truth for you and me. Jesus identified His role in this way: "But when he, the Spirit of truth, comes, he will guide you into all truth. He will not speak on his own; he will speak only what he hears, and he will tell you what is yet to come."

The Bible is a wonderful book of history and poetry and prophecy and ceremony. Anyone can be blessed by just reading this truly magnificent piece of literature that spans the years of human history. But there is a unique blessing that is reserved for those who prayerfully, earnestly, and humbly approach it by faith as the truth, seeking to go past the surface reading into the deeper meaning. And it is impossible to reach this deeper level of understanding and blessing without the Holy Spirit's guidance. How do you approach God's Word?

My Heart's Cry

THE FACE OF GOD

We have seen his glory, the glory of the one and only
Son who came from the Father, full of grace and truth.

JOHN 1:14, NIV

Today countless people look for a god within themselves or in crystals or in trees or in a former life or in some statue or in a religious experience or in the stars. But John declares the awesome truth that the glory of God is not confined in any of those things, just as it is no longer confined in a Tabernacle or as a cloud or fire. Instead "the Word became flesh and lived for a while among us. We have seen his glory, the glory of the one and only Son who came from the Father, full of grace and truth."

John is saying emphatically, "I have seen Him!

"I've seen Him when He was alone.

"I've seen Him when He was surrounded by a crowd of people.

"I've seen Him dead, buried, risen, and ascended. And in every situation I have seen Him full of grace and full of truth! I have seen the face of God—in the face of Jesus!"

Just Give Me Jesus

CREATED IN GOD'S IMAGE

God created man in his own image, in the mage of God
he created him; male and female he created them.
GENESIS 1:27, NIV

Nothing like man had ever existed in the universe prior to his creation. Through the power of God's Word, man was brought into existence from nothing. The difference between man and all other life forms is that man was created in the image of God.

By creating man in His own image, God fixed a gulf between animals and man that will never be bridged. Animals always have been and always will be animals. Man always has been and always will be man. The fossil evidence confirms this. No one has ever found the "missing link," and no one ever will because it's missing! It doesn't exist! Since Creation, approximately ten billion human beings have been born, yet there is not a single recorded case of one ever being genetically less than a human being. Man was created in God's own image with a capacity to know the Creator in a personal relationship. Do you know Him?

God's Story

GOD LOVES EVEN ME!

"I will never leave you nor forsake you."

HEBREWS 13:5, NKJV

In the midst of our suffering, it can often be difficult to glimpse the glory to come. Suffering is so immediate and can seem so permanent that we can easily lose sight of the big picture. The pain can be so crushing and our hearts can be so broken that we just don't understand why! *Why me?* Whenever that question tends to fill my mind, I hear God whisper to my heart, "Anne, why *not* you? Just trust Me! Trust Me to be with you. Trust Me to bring you through. Trust Me to be enough for you. Trust Me—because I love you!"

When I don't understand why, I trust Him because . . . God loves even me!

Are you hurt because you've thought that if God truly loved you, you would be exempt from pain and problems and pressure? Lay your hurts at His nail-pierced feet—and just trust Him because He loves even you!

Why?

AUGUST 18

EQUIPPED TO SERVE

There are different kinds of gifts, but the same Spirit.
There are different kinds of service, but the same Lord.

1 CORINTHIANS 12:4–5, NIV

What God commands you and me to do, He equips us for. It's that simple!

If you want to discover your spiritual gifts, start obeying God. Responding to His command with "I can't" is invalid, because He will never command you to do something that He has not equipped and empowered you to do. As you serve Him, you will find that He has given you the gifts that are necessary to follow through in obedience. Any of them. All of them. And if you lack any that you need, God will bring people alongside you who have the gifts that you don't. Working together, you will accomplish the task to the glory of God.

And that's the body of Christ! That's the church. Individual members of the family, each obeying his or her call, exercising the particular gifts the Spirit has given, so that our work is not in vain but produces eternal results. So . . . get to work! You're equipped!

Just Give Me Jesus

AUGUST 19

THE TRAGEDY OF CAIN'S LIFE

Cain went out from the LORD's presence
and lived in the land of Nod, east of Eden.
GENESIS 4:16, NIV

Cain had been created by God. He had been created with life from God. He had been created for God. And now he was separated from God. Unconfessed sin and rebellion make a person so miserable in the presence of a holy, righteous God that the sin must either be confessed and cleansed or the sinner must leave God's presence.

Cain's tragic life illustrates the hard lesson that guilt is our friend if it drives us to God. However, if we refuse to turn to God in repentance and confession, guilt will drive us away from God to our own destruction. Cain's bitterness that was rooted in resentment and rebellion bore wicked fruit in his family for generations to follow. Cain's sin, left to take its own natural course, intensified with each generation until the entire civilization of the world in his day was ravaged by it.

What sin in your life—if left unchecked—will ravage the life of your children?

God's Story

GOD WANTS US TO ASK!

If we know that He hears us, whatever we ask, we know that we have the petitions that we have asked of Him.

1 JOHN 5:15, NKJV

During the days of Ezekiel, God poured out His heart and shared what He wanted to do for His beloved people. Then He revealed an astonishing fact: "I will yet for this be enquired of by the house of Israel, to do it for them" (Eze. 36:37, KJV). God was waiting to be asked!

My mother has said that if there are any tears shed in heaven, they are going to be shed over all the answers to prayer for which no one ever bothered to ask! What blessing is God waiting to give you, but you haven't asked Him for it?

Why does He wait for us to ask? Maybe He wants us to acknowledge our need of Him. Maybe it's one way of getting our attention. Maybe it's the only way we will know when the answer comes that it comes from Him, and we don't credit ourselves or someone else for it.

My Heart's Cry

LISTENING TO GOD

Direct my steps by Your word,
and let no iniquity have dominion over me.

PSALM 119:133, NKJV

"Noah was a righteous man, blameless among the people of his time, and he walked with God" (Gen. 6:9, NIV). Noah was right with God when everyone else was wrong. Noah was blameless among the people of his time when every other person was to blame for every kind of evil. Noah walked with God when the entire world followed in Cain's rebellious footsteps and ran away from God. Yet Noah's attitude seemed to be so confident it was as though he considered the whole world to be crazy while he was the only one who was sane! Surely he received much-needed strength and encouragement from his wife and three sons, but his confidence came from listening to what God had to say.

Noah listened to God as he walked with God, cultivating the awareness of His Presence. Are you a good listener?

God's Story

PRAISING JESUS IS CONTAGIOUS!

*"To him who sits on the throne and to the Lamb
be praise and honor and glory and power for ever and ever!"*

REVELATION 5:13, NIV

The apostle John gives us a thrilling glimpse into a universal celebration that one day we are going to participate in. He describes four living creatures who surround the throne on which Jesus reigns supreme. These living creatures never stop saying: "Holy, holy, holy is the Lord God Almighty, who was, and is, and is to come" (Rev. 4:8, NIV). While the living creatures proclaim glory, the twenty-four elders fall down and worship. And as the elders praise, millions of angels join in the chorus, singing in a loud voice, "Worthy is the Lamb, who was slain, to receive power and wealth and wisdom and strength and honor and glory and praise!" Then John describes the entire universe beginning to roar in the continuous acclamation of Christ as every creature in heaven and on earth and under the earth and on the sea sings: 'To the Lord, the Lamb be praise and honor and glory and power for ever and ever!'"

So . . . who is praising Christ because you are?

My Heart's Cry

AUGUST 23

WAIT FOR THE LORD

Wait for the LORD and keep his way.
He will exalt you to inherit the land.

PSALM 37:34, NIV

"On the seventeenth day of the seventh month the ark came to rest on the mountains of Ararat" (Gen. 8:4, NIV). When Noah first gazed out of the window, drinking in the warmth of the sunshine and breathing the clean, fresh air, it must have looked like he was on an island in the midst of a vast lake. But as the water continued to recede, what did he think when he realized he was on top of a mountain range seventeen thousand feet high?

As Noah became aware of the gradual yet drastic changes taking place in his circumstances, he must have feared what they would mean to his everyday life. He was an old man to be starting out in a new job requiring a new home and a totally new environment. But like the psalmist, Noah knew he should "wait for the LORD and keep his way." He had to keep trusting that the same God Who had saved him from the storm of judgment that had "cut off" the wicked would enable him to inherit the "land" of his new life.

God's Story

HE IS PRECIOUS

You come to him, the living Stone. . . .
Now to you who believe, this stone is precious.
1 PETER 2:4, 7, NIV

Have you ever denied the Lord?

Denied Him with your silence?

Denied Him with your behavior?

Denied Him by calling yourself a Christian
yet not acting like one?

Denied Him by the priorities and plans and
people and places in your life that are
Christ-less?

If you have denied Jesus—and surely all of us
have in some way—then you know something of
the price Peter paid in shame and humiliation for
his denial. Instead of repressing your shame and
guilt, will you confess it to the Lord so that you can
experience the same forgiveness and restoration
that Peter did? When you do, you can share the
testimony with Peter and the saints down through
the ages who know from their own experience that
He is precious! "Speak, LORD, for your servant is
listening" (1 Sam 3:9, NIV).

Just Give Me Jesus

PLUGGED INTO THE POWER SOURCE

*In Your hand is power and might; in Your hand
it is to make great and to give strength to all.*
1 CHRONICLES 29:12, NKJV

The crowning jewel of Creation was man himself. He was created for a distinct purpose. If the purpose is lived out, life is fulfilling. If the purpose is rejected or ignored, life will never be what it was meant to be.

A light bulb is a simple glass globe. If placed on a desk or table, it is meaningless as well as useless. But if it is fitted into a lamp and plugged into a power source, it fulfills its purpose for existence, taking on meaning as a source of light that is useful for daily living.

Apart from the Creator's purpose, you and I are like a light bulb lying in a meaningless, useless state. We need to fit into the Creator's original design, plugging into the power source—our relationship with Him—if our lives are to be what they were meant to be.

God's Story

A PLATFORM OF SUFFERING

*"My grace is sufficient for you,
for my power is made perfect in weakness."*

2 CORINTHIANS 12:9, NIV

The apostle Paul went through a period of intense suffering that he described as being impaled with a spike! He testified that three times he pleaded with God to remove the suffering, but his prayer was unanswered. When he must have cried out through clenched teeth, *"Why?"* God reassured him, "My grace is sufficient for you, for my power is made perfect in weakness." Paul's response indicates he caught sight of the big picture when he responded, "Therefore I will boast all the more gladly about my weaknesses, so that Christ's power may rest on me. That is why, for Christ's sake, I delight in weaknesses, in insults, in hardships, in persecutions, in difficulties. For when I am weak, then I am strong" (2 Cor. 12:9–10, NIV).

What kinds of trials have caused you to suffer? Could it be God has given you a platform of suffering from which you can be a witness of His power and grace to those who are watching? *Why?*

AUGUST 27

LITTLE CLAY POTS

You are our Father; we are the clay, and You our potter;
and all we are the work of Your hand.

ISAIAH 64:8, NKJV

The principle that suffering leads to glory is illustrated in Scripture by a vivid description of clay on the Potter's wheel—clay that was once cracked, shattered, and broken, clay that was totally useless and ugly. The Potter took the clay and broke it down even further, grinding it into dust then moistening it with water before He put it on His wheel and began to remake it into a vessel pleasing to Himself. The cracks and chips and broken pieces disappeared as the clay became soft and pliable to the Potter's touch.

But the clay was still soft and weak, the color dull and drab. So the Potter placed the vessel into the fiery kiln, carefully keeping His eye on it as He submitted it to the raging heat. At a time He alone determined was sufficient, the Potter withdrew the pot from the furnace. The blazing heat had radically transformed into a vessel of strength and glorious, multicolored beauty.

You and I are just little clay pots destined for glory!

Why?

THE JOY OF WORKING TOGETHER

Whatever you do in word or deed,
do all in the name of the Lord Jesus.

COLOSSIANS 3:17, NKJV

What task has God assigned you? Has He assigned you to . . .

establish a home,

strengthen a marriage,

serve a church,

teach in a classroom,

or comfort in a sick room?

Check your attitude toward the assignment. Do you grumble and complain about it? Do you neglect and ignore it? Do you resent and reject it? Or do you enjoy fulfilling it as your service unto the Lord? God wants you and me to enjoy our service to Him, whatever it may be. And He also wants us to discuss each detail with Him as we do the work. One of His pleasures, as well as ours, is the joy of working together as we complete the task. Often, the more difficult the task, the greater the joy because it enables us to see the power of God and just what He can do in and through and for us.

God's Story

AUGUST 29

IT'S TIME TO SIMPLY TRUST

"Did I not tell you that if you believed,
you would see the glory of God?"

JOHN 11:40, NIV

Having commanded the stone to be rolled away from the place where Lazarus was buried, Jesus challenged Martha not only to obedience but to expectant faith: "Did I not tell you that if you believed, you would see the glory of God?" (11:40). In essence, He was saying, "It's time to place all of your small, mustard seed–sized faith in Me and My promise to you."

Martha had said she had faith. She intellectually believed what Jesus had said. But Martha needed to make the transition from faith to trust. Because while belief is the consent of the mind and faith is a choice of the will, trust is a commitment of the heart.

The time had come for Martha to put her faith into action by surrendering all of her hopeful expectations and heartfelt longings and practical common sense and simply trust Him. And the time has come for you to simply trust Him. Trust HIM!

Why?

THE SPIRIT OF TRUTH

"When he the Spirit of truth, comes,
he will guide you into all truth."

JOHN 16:13, NIV

The Holy Spirit is so identified with the Bible, one of His names is Truth! In fact, Peter reveals that the Holy Spirit is the inspirational Author of the Old Testament Scriptures. (2 Pet. 1:20–21) And Paul wrote to Timothy, encouraging him to stay in the Scriptures because, "all Scripture is God-breathed," referring once again to the Spirit-inspired Word of God (2 Tim. 3:16, NIV).

Have you been trying to work up some kind of emotional feeling? If you lack "it," have you *felt* you didn't have the Holy Spirit? The Holy Spirit is the Spirit of Truth, which means He always works according to and through the Word of God whether you *feel* Him or not. Have you been seeking some ecstatic experience, thinking that would be the Holy Spirit? Remember that He never acts independently; He always works through *the* Truth—the living Word of God, Who is Jesus, and the written Word of God, which is your Bible.

Just Give Me Jesus

A LIFE THAT WORKS

*There is a way that seems right to a man,
but its end is the way of death.*

PROVERBS 14:12, NKJV

The first seventeen verses of Genesis 9 are a
direct quotation in God's own words giving
principles for you and me and the entire human race
to live by. If we want to live a life that works,
overcoming the weakness that resides in all of us, we
must heed these principles. If we do not want to
heed these principles, we have that freedom, but we
will never live a life that works as it was created to
work in the beginning. It would be similar to having
a new computer with a Pentium processor but using
it only as a typewriter. It would do the job, but it
wouldn't even come close to fulfilling its potential. If
we do not heed God's principles for our lives, you
and I can exist on this planet yet not even come close
to fulfilling our potential or experiencing the
abundant life God intended for us.

So . . . for your own good, read God's Word and
live by God's principles and enjoy a life that works!

God's Story

September

God's Word makes a lasting impact—
because it's powerful!

HIS OFFER

I am the LORD, I do not change.

MALACHI 3:6, NKJV

Jesus, the Living Logos, is enduringly the same today as He always has been: "The same was in the beginning with God" (John 1:2, NKJV). There was no personality change in this Person from the beginning of time until John's day to our day to the last day of human history on into eternity.

The One Who spoke all things into existence and then transformed Planet Earth from a formless, empty, dark, water-submerged blob dangling in space to a beautiful place that reflected His own image is the same Person Who has power today to transform your life and mine.

The One Who offered all men of Noah's day salvation from the storm of His judgment if they would come into the ark is the same Person today Who offers all men salvation from His eternal judgment if they come into Him at the cross. So . . . extend His offer to someone you know.

Just Give Me Jesus

GOD IS ACTIVE IN BIG WAYS

He counts the number of the stars;
He calls them by name.

PSALM 147:4, NKJV

Astronomers estimate there are more than 100 billion galaxies. And each galaxy has more than 100 billion stars! And each of those hundreds of billions of stars was personally hung in space by the Creator Who has not only numbered them all but knows each of them by name! The very first words of Genesis tell us, "In the beginning, God created the heavens. . . ." I can't conceive of any activity much bigger than that!

What big things are you facing? A big decision about a career change or a child's schooling or a marriage proposal? A big commitment like buying a new house or beginning a new job or becoming a new parent? A big responsibility such as caring for elderly parents or supervising an office staff or being the sole provider for your family?

God is active in big ways! Nothing is too big for Him.

God's Story

STREETS OF GOLD

The great street of the city was of pure gold,
like transparent glass.
REVELATION 21:21, NIV

The streets of our heavenly home are not only made of pure gold but, amazingly and almost incomprehensively, they are also described as being as transparent as glass. Surely gold that is polished until it looks like transparent glass would function as a mirror.

The Bible tells us that when we get to Heaven all of our sins and flaws will fall away, and we will be like Jesus. With our unique personalities and characteristics, every single one of us is going to perfectly reflect the character of Christ. And as we walk on streets that reflect like mirrors, every step we take and every move we make is going to bring glory to Him.

Heaven: My Father's House

GOD'S POWERFUL WORD

The word of God is living and active.
Sharper than any double-edged sword;
it penetrates even to dividing soul and spirit.

HEBREWS 4:12, NIV

When we know the truth and we are presented with that which is false, we will instinctively recognize it. Measuring philosophies or theologies or books or doctrines or counsel by the Word of God is like exposing the crookedness of a stick by placing a straight stick beside it. The ultimate compliment an audience can pay me is to bring their Bibles and follow along as I speak so they can double-check what I say against what God says. I am authentic as a Bible teacher only in proportion to my faithfulness to God's Word.

And in order to give God's Word out so that others can hear His voice in their ears, I must—it's not an option—I must read it, study it, understand it, and live by it. And when I do, His Word makes a lasting impact and bears eternal fruit, because it's powerful.

My Heart's Cry

GOD MADE VISIBLE

Salvation is found in no one else,
for there is no other name under heaven given
to men by which we must be saved.

ACTS 4:12, NIV

Who do you know who says we can each have our own religion as long as we're sincere? Does that person put a guilt trip on you for what he or she describes as a dogmatic, narrow-minded, intolerant, and exclusive faith? But the Gospel wasn't our idea, was it? Jesus Himself declared, "I am the way and the truth and the life. *No one* comes to the Father except through me" (John 14:6, NIV). We must come to God through Him or we don't come at all. The Bible says emphatically that "salvation is found in *no one* else, for there is *no* other name under heaven given to men by which we must be saved." Just the name Jesus.

And Who is Jesus? He is God Himself made visible to all. Praise God! You and I are not condemned to live in the darkness because He has turned on the Light! Praise God for just giving us Jesus!

Just Give Me Jesus

GOD'S GUARANTEE

"I will pray the Father, and He will give you another Helper, that He may abide with you forever."

JOHN 14:16, NKJV

The same Spirit that hovered over the surface of the deep in the second verse of the Bible is the same Spirit that fully indwelt Jesus Christ. (John 3:34) In John 14 Jesus speaks of Him as the Spirit of truth, (John 14:17) because He always works through the truth, which is incarnate in Christ and written in the Scriptures. (2 Pet. 1:21–22) He is also referred to as the Counselor because He gives wisdom, direction for living, and understanding of the truth. (John 14:16) And He is called the Holy Spirit because He is totally separate from sin. (John 14:26)

This wonderful Spirit of God is available to live within you when you repent of your sin and, by faith, invite Jesus Christ to come into your life as your Lord and Savior. (John 14:17) In fact, without the "seal" of His Presence in your life, you have no eternal credibility with the Father. (Eph. 1:13) But with the "seal" of His Presence you have the guarantee of a heavenly home and all the blessings of God.

God's Story

THE CLICK OF THE PRUNING SHEARS

*"This is to my Father's glory, that you bear much fruit,
showing yourselves to be my disciples."*

JOHN 15:8, NIV

The firm "click" of the Gardener's pruning
shears can be heard in our lives when . . .

we are confined to a hospital room,

we are fired from a job,

we are moved to a new place, surrounded by
strangers,

we are isolated in a new job, surrounded by
unbelievers.

Your purpose, and mine, is to bring glory to
God. Jesus reiterated this purpose as He concluded
His challenge to the disciples to be fruitful in
service: "This is to my Father's glory, that you bear
much fruit, showing yourselves to be my disciples."

You will not bear much fruit unless and until you
submit to the cutting and clipping of the Gardener.
Therefore, when you resist His "gardening" in your
life, what you are really doing is refusing to glorify
God and therefore aborting the very purpose for your
existence. Solemn thoughts, aren't they?

My Heart's Cry

LOVE HIM FOR WHO HE IS

As the bridegroom rejoices over the bride,
so shall your God rejoice over you.

ISAIAH 62:5. NKJV

God loves for us to come to Him and ask Him for things. But I wonder what kind of relationship I would have with my husband if I shared only about fifteen minutes a day with him and spent the first minute or two thanking him for what he had done for me and the rest of the time asking him to do something else for me! I doubt we would have a very good relationship! My husband wants me to love him simply for who he is. And Jesus Christ, Who is my heavenly Husband, also wants to be loved for Who He is. Not just for what He has done, or may do, but for Who He is in Himself. Would you make time each day to praise Jesus for Who He is? Read the Bible, gleaning His attributes that you might live your life in praise of Who He is.

The Vision of His Glory

GOD'S LAMB

He . . . did not spare His own Son,
but delivered Him up for us all.

ROMANS 8:32, NKJV

Abraham's faith was tested when God told him to take his son, his only son, the son he loved, and offer him as a sacrifice. And Abraham did. Abraham bound Isaac to the altar and raised his knife to slay him in strict obedience to God's Word. Just before the gleaming knife plunged down, God leaned out of heaven and urgently commanded, "Abraham! Abraham! . . . Do not lay a hand on the boy," and Isaac's life was spared! Abraham looked around; caught in the thicket nearby was a ram. After cutting Isaac loose, Abraham took the ram and offered it on the altar.

As God's Son, God's only Son, the Son He loved, hung on the Cross, the knife of God's fierce wrath against sin was lifted, and there was no one to stay the Father's hand. Instead, "He . . . did not spare his own Son, but gave him up for us all." Jesus was God's Lamb and our Substitute Who endured the full force of God's wrath for your sins and mine.

Just Give Me Jesus

AN EXTREME MAKE-OVER

Then He who sat on the throne said,
"Behold, I make all things new."
REVELATION 21:5, NKJV

"Then God said, 'Let the land produce vegetation: seed-bearing plants and trees on the land that bear fruit with seed in it, according to their various kinds.' And it was so" (Gen. 1:11, NIV).

I wonder what it would have been like to watch the bleak, barren, desolate planet suddenly softened with . . .

> spidery ferns,
>> exotic orchids,
>>> weeping willow trees,
>>>> carpeted fields of grass,

until it was breathtakingly beautiful!

What does the land of your life look like? Is it drab and devoid of the real beauty of joy and happiness? Is it desolate from lack of love? Perhaps it is even ugly because of the scars of sin and suffering. If God, through the power of His Word, transformed Planet Earth into something that was beautiful, He can do the same for you. Ask Him for an extreme make-over!

God's Story

GOD'S PRIMARY PURPOSE

I will fear no evil, for you are with me;
your rod and your staff, they comfort me.
PSALM 23:4, NIV

Trusting God to accomplish His primary purpose through pain was eloquently expressed by the widow of Todd Beamer. Todd was a passenger on the fateful United Flight 93 when it was hijacked by suicide bombers on September 11, 2001. He and other passengers overpowered the hijackers, but were unable to prevent the plane from a nosedive crash into a vacant field in Pennsylvania, so September 11, 2001, was the date of Todd Beamer's entrance into heaven. Lisa Beamer gave us a snapshot of her faith that is being developed through suffering when she told an interviewer, "God says, 'I knew on September 10, and I could have stopped it, but I have a plan for greater good than you can ever imagine.' I don't know God's plan, and, honestly, right now I don't like it very much. But I trust that He is true to His promise in Romans 8:28."

Thank you, Lisa, for trusting God when you don't understand why!

Why?

IN HIS PRESENCE . . . FOREVER!

I did not see a temple in the city, because the
Lord God Almighty and the Lamb are its temple.

The Greek word for "temple" is, in this case, the same word used for the "Most Holy Place," which was the inner sanctuary of the ancient Israelites' tabernacle, and later the temple. It was the place where God was said to dwell. The high priest could only enter once a year to sprinkle the sacrificed animals' blood on the mercy seat in order to make atonement for the sin of God's people. The Book of Hebrews teaches us that today "we have confidence to enter the Most Holy Place by the blood of Jesus, by a new and living way opened for us through the curtain, that is, his body" (Heb. 10:19–20, NIV). In other words, through the death and broken body of Jesus Christ on the cross, you and I have been given access to the presence of God when we approach Him by faith in prayer.

In our heavenly home, we will not just have occasional access to the presence of God; we will live in His presence! For all eternity!

Heaven: My Father's House

THE SIGN OF A RAINBOW

This is the sign of the covenant which I have established between Me and all flesh that is on the earth.

GENESIS 9:17, NKJV

"I have set my rainbow in the clouds, and it will be the sign of the covenant between me and the earth. . . . Never again will the waters become a flood to destroy all life" (Gen. 9:12–16, NIV).

As God explained to Noah the meaning of the rainbow, surely peace and gratitude flooded Noah's heart as he knew, based on God's Word alone, that he was safe and secure.

God gave Noah the sign of a rainbow to symbolize His covenant. When the thunder clouds rolled and the rain began to fall and Noah was consciously aware of sin in his life and the lives of others, he was to look up and see the rainbow. The purpose was not for him to remember God's covenant but to remember that God remembered His commitment to the human race. And God remembers that He is still committed to us.

God's Story

FRUIT IN MY LIFE

"I am the vine; you are the branches."

JOHN 15:5, NIV

Why is it that Christians go running around, measuring the abundance of each other's fruit as well as their own, reading books on fruitfulness, going to seminars about greater fruitfulness, when it's really not their concern? Before you start to protest, let me assure you I desire with all of my heart to bear much fruit for the glory of God.

But the fruit in my life is His concern, not mine. My concern is to make sure of three things: that as a potential fruit-bearing branch, I am connected to the Vine and keep that connection clean and unobstructed; that I submit to the cultivation of the Vinedresser, which primarily involves His pruning in my life; and that I communicate with Him my heart's desire.

Instead of examining your fruit, would you examine the branch?

My Heart's Cry

SHOWERED WITH BLESSINGS

From the fullness of his grace
we have all received one blessing after another.

JOHN 1:16, NIV

As children of God, we are the primary recipients of His blessing. Regardless of our past failures or present shortcomings, our relationship with Jesus Christ ensures that "from the fullness of his grace we have all received one blessing after another."

When the Mediterranean Sea evaporates or runs low, the Atlantic Ocean rushes in at the Strait of Gibraltar to replenish it and keep it full. When you and I are related to Jesus Christ, our strength and wisdom and peace and joy and love and hope may run out, but His life rushes in to keep us filled to the brim—not because of anything we have or have not done, but just because of Him we are showered with blessings.

Just Give Me Jesus

BEAUTIFUL IN CHRIST

He has made everything beautiful in its time.

ECCLESIASTES 3:11, NKJV

"The land produced vegetation: plants bearing seed according to their kinds and trees bearing fruit with seed in it according to their kinds. And God saw that it was good" (Gen. 1:12, NIV).

Through the power of His Word, God brought beauty to the barrenness and added color to the drabness. God did not create anything new. He just called it forth from what was already present, because apparently that which was necessary for plant life was in the soil.

It doesn't matter if your life has always been dry, barren, bleak, desolate, and ugly, or if it has become that way because of some tragedy or crisis. If you submit your life to the skillful touch of the Creator, He has the power to transform you into someone who is beautiful—beautiful not because of a toned physique or flawless skin or a perfect figure or manageable hair but because the life of Christ radiates from within you: His joy sparkling from your eyes, His love lighting up your face.

God's Story

THE MYSTERY OF GOD

In the beginning, God . . .

GENESIS 1:1, NKJV

Someone has said that if God were small enough for us to understand, He would not be big enough to save us. Yet the Bible is God's revelation of Himself to us. And the revelation is true . . .

At the birth of time and space and human history, against the inky blackness of the universe and the shadowy mysteriousness of eternity, the character of God shone forth with the radiant beauty of a full moon in a cloudless night sky. Even the casual reader of the creation account in Genesis can easily identify . . .

His unequaled power as He called into existence that which had no existence,

His unlimited sovereignty as He took counsel with Himself and decided to create man in His own image,

and His unsearchable goodness that was revealed when He created Adam, the first man.

In what way have you glimpsed the character of God today? Would you praise Him for it?

Why?

ENRICHING THE FAMILY

We were all baptized by one Spirit into one body . . .
and we were all given the one Spirit to drink.

1 CORINTHIANS 12:13, NIV

When you and I received the Holy Spirit into our lives, we became members of the larger body of Christ that includes other believers. Perhaps without realizing it, at the moment of conversion, we became part of the family of God; Jesus is the Head, and other believers are our brothers and sisters. Paul describes this new identity as being "baptized by one Spirit into one body." But the new privilege of belonging to God's family brings with it new responsibilities to care for and build up the other family members. For that purpose, the Holy Spirit gives us each gifts that enable us to be contributing family members. These gifts are not natural talents although they can enhance what we have developed ourselves. These gifts are supernatural and only come from the Spirit at His discretion. (1 Cor. 12:11)

What is your spiritual gift? Ask the Holy Spirit to reveal what it is so you can use it to enrich the family!

Just Give Me Jesus

BITTER OR BLESSED?

Blessed is he whose
transgression is forgiven, whose sin is covered.

PSALM 32:1, NKJV

———————

Your heavenly Father has been waiting for you to come home to Him, waiting for you to confess your sin of resentment and rebellion, waiting to celebrate the joy and love and pleasure He wants you to have in relationship with Him. Don't make excuses; don't rationalize your bitterness. Go to God; ask Him to cleanse you of your sin. Ask Him to uproot your bitterness. Invite Him into your life to take control of everything, including past memories of abandonment or abuse or adultery, present circumstances of injury or injustice, and future dreams and disappointments.

Follow the example of the psalmist, who wrote, "I will confess my transgression to the LORD" (Ps. 32:5, NIV).

"Blessed is he whose transgression is forgiven, whose sin is covered."

Wouldn't you rather be blessed than bitter?

God's Story

HEAVENLY ASPHALT

The great street of the city was of pure gold,
like transparent glass.
REVELATION 21:21, NIV

If the apostle John hasn't already conveyed to us that My Father's House is spectacular, his description of the streets surely does. But I wonder if there is a subtle message to us contained in his description—a message that my wise mother, with her characteristic humor, pointed out to me when she dryly exclaimed that you can tell what God thinks of gold because He paves the streets of heaven with it! Gold is really just heavenly asphalt! In other words, there are many things down here on earth that we give a top priority to, which in eternity will be inconsequential and insignificant.

It's sobering to contemplate how much time, effort, sacrifice, compromise, and attention we give to acquiring and increasing our supply of something that is totally insignificant in eternity. What are *your* priorities? As you live them out, will they have eternal value and significance?

Heaven: My Father's House

LISTENING WITH OUR EYES

*They received the message with great eagerness
and examined the Scriptures every day to see
if what Paul said was true.*

ACTS 17:11, NIV

Following the resurrection and ascension of
Jesus Christ, His disciples fanned out all over the
known world, telling people they could now be
reconciled with God through faith in Jesus Christ.
How were the religious faithful to know if this
was true?

A fascinating glimpse is given to us when the
apostle Paul, who had started heated debates in
practically every city where he preached the Gospel,
slipped into the little town of Berea. As was his
custom, he went straight to the synagogue in order to
share the wonderful good news that the Messiah had
come. This time when he preached, "they received
the message with great eagerness and examined the
Scriptures every day to see if what Paul said was true."

We will recognize our Shepherd's voice when we
listen with our eyes on the pages of our Bibles.

My Heart's Cry

WITH GOD, YOU'RE A MAJORITY

He who has begun a good work in you
will complete it until the day of Jesus Christ.

PHILIPPIANS 1:6, NKJV

God is looking for a few good men and
women. Men and women who are willing
to go against the current of popular opinion,
to hold firm convictions in a world where
"anything goes,"
to speak the truth when it is not politically correct,
to walk with God when everyone else is running
away from Him.
God is looking for those who believe
that what He says is more important than
what anyone else says,
that what He thinks is more important than
what anyone else thinks,
that what He wants is more important than
what anyone else wants.
that His will is more important than their own.
God is looking for another Noah. Another
Meshach. Another Shadrach. Another Abednego.
One person with God is not alone but a majority!

God's Story

"TREES OF RIGHTEOUSNESS"

That they may be called trees of righteousness,
the planting of the LORD, that He may be glorified.
ISAIAH 61:3, NKJV

When I was growing up in the mountains of North Carolina, every Sunday afternoon, weather permitting, my parents, my siblings, and I would go hiking. Inevitably, our climbs would take us to the ridge where the trees were so enormous we could all hold hands and still not be able to encircle the trunks. When I asked my mother why the trees were so much larger on the ridge than anywhere else, she replied that it was because the winds were the strongest and the storms were the fiercest on the ridge. With nothing to shelter the trees from the full brunt of nature's wrath, they either broke and fell, or they became incredibly strong and resilient.

God plants you and me in our faith as tender saplings then grows us up into "trees of righteousness," using the elements of adversity to make us strong. And He leads us to endure, not just somehow, but triumphantly as we choose to praise Him, regardless of the storms swirling within us or the winds howling outside of us.

My Heart's Cry

GOD IS GREAT—STILL!

The steps of a good man are ordered by the LORD,
and He delights in his way.

PSALM 37:23, NKJV

Before the Flood, God had said, "Come into the ark" (Gen. 7:1, NKJV). The clear implication was that God was already inside, inviting Noah to join Him there. After the Flood, when God said, "Come out of the ark" (Gen. 8:16, NIV), the implication is that He had left and was asking Noah to follow. The great God of the Exodus Who led His people out of bondage to slavery in Egypt—that same great God led Noah, his wife, his sons, his sons' wives, and all the animals out of the ark!

God's greatness has not been diluted in any way over the years of time. He is just as great today as He has been in the past. So why do you think He cannot lead you out of trouble? Why would you think He cannot lead your entire life so that you find peace and fulfillment? Why do you think He is unable to lead your children in the right direction that will be pleasing to Him and good for them? God is great—still!

God's Story

BREAKING THE SILENCE

*You have purified your souls in obeying
the truth through the Spirit.*

1 PETER 1:22, NKJV

Is God silent in your life? Could it be that He has given you truth to which you have not responded obediently? Has He given you truth through a Bible study,

or your pastor's sermon,

or your daily devotions,

or an inspirational book,

or a godly friend,

that you have yet to apply and obey? Have you been frustrated because the Bible doesn't seem to make sense to you? And when you pray, is it as though your prayers hit the ceiling of your room and bounce back? Have you felt as though God has abandoned you? If so, you need to go back to the last thing you can remember that He told you and act on it. If you can't remember, just return to the cross by faith. In prayer, confess your sin of disobedience whether it was willful or not. Ask God to break His silence in your life.

Just Give Me Jesus

FRUIT FOR YOUR CHILDREN

The fruit of the Spirit is love, joy, peace, patience,
kindness, goodness, faithfulness, gentleness and self-control.

GALATIANS 5:22, NIV

God's Word describes the characteristics of Christ that are to be revealed in our lives as spiritual "fruit." Love, joy, peace, patience, kindness, goodness, faithfulness, gentleness, and self-control is the fruit of the Spirit that ought to be bountifully present in our homes. What kind of "fruit" are your children eating within your home? Does their "diet" consist of nagging, complaining, anger, bickering, gossip, selfishness, and rudeness? Or are they learning to be loving when someone is not lovable, to have joy when life is not fun, to have peace in the midst of pressure, to be kind when treated roughly? How easy do you make it for your children to "eat healthy"?

Our homes should be places of rich, bountiful, moral, and spiritual teaching for our children. But that is only possible if we ourselves are moral and spiritual people. Are you?

God's Story

OPEN YOUR HEART TO GOD

Search me, O God, and know my heart;
try me, and know my anxieties;
and see if there is any wicked way in me.

PSALM 139:23–24, NKJV

Have you erected a shield around your heart?
A shield . . .

of pride

or doubt

or shame

or anger?

Did you think that if you opened your heart and
let God see inside, that He would blame you for what
you have or haven't done? Or rebuke you for your
lack of faith?

You and I can be so foolish! Why do we think
we can hide our feelings from God? Why would we
want to hide our feelings from God? Would you
open up your heart and show it to Him? Let Him
see exactly how you feel and what you think. Don't
hide it or repress it or cover it up or pretend it's not
there. Just pour it all out to Him, and then wait
expectantly for His response.

Why?

WE ARE WONDERFULLY MADE

I praise you because I am fearfully and wonderfully made.

PSALM 139:14, NIV

We can only imagine the concentrated thoughts that occupied the divine Mind and the gentle, skillful touch of the divine Hand that first shaped man from the dust. Where did the Creator begin? Did He start with a skeletal frame? Did He then cover it with an outside layer of skin, which at no place is thicker than three-sixteenths of an inch, is packed with nerve endings to enable man to feel the outside world, and is virtually waterproof? Into the skin stretched over the frame did He next place the heart that pumps seventy-two times a minute, forty million times a year? When did He hang the lungs in their sealed compartments so that the rivers of blood necessary for life can deposit the carbon dioxide and pick up oxygen to be carried to every single one of the more than twenty-six trillion cells in the body? Truly, we are fearfully and wonderfully and lovingly and personally created by an awe-inspiring, loving Creator!

God's Story

WILLING TO BE WHOLE

"Do you want to get well?"

JOHN 5:6, NIV

Jesus didn't ask the man beside the pool of Bethesda, "Do you *need* to get well?" But, "Do you *want* to get well?" There was no preliminary introduction or social niceties or even casual conversation, just a Stranger asking a question that would seem to have had a very obvious answer. Surely, without question, anyone who was a paralytic would *want* to be able to walk.

But Jesus knew that it's easy for physical weakness and mental depression and a lifetime of hopelessness to rob a man of his willingness to do anything about it. It would be less demanding in many ways for the man to be carried about by others. His paralysis absolved him from taking responsibility in life.

Jesus knows one of the greatest barriers to our faith is often our *unwillingness* to be made whole— our unwillingness to live without excuse for our spiritual smallness and immaturity. And so the question He asked was very relevant then and still is today: "Do you want to get well?"

Just Give Me Jesus

SOARING HIGHER

*Even if you should suffer
for righteousness' sake, you are blessed.*
1 PETER 3:14, NKJV

Within a period of eighteen months, I went through a cluster of storms that left me emotionally gasping for breath. From Hurricane Fran, which downed 102 trees in our yard, to the fire that consumed my husband's dental office, to my son, Jonathan's, cancer and surgery, to my parents' increasingly fragile health and multiple hospitalizations. I reeled from one emergency or crisis to another.

Looking back over that eighteen-month period, my confident conclusion is that God allowed the storms of suffering to increase and intensify in my life because He wanted me to soar higher in my relationship with Him—to fall deeper in love with Him.

Faith that triumphantly soars is possible only when the winds of life are contrary to personal comfort. That kind of faith is God's ultimate purpose for our lives: Trust Him!

Why?

October

You were deliberately planned—
to be filled with God Himself.

JESUS IS ALIVE!

He is not here, but is risen!

LUKE 24:6, NKJV

It was early Sunday morning before dawn. An elite, handpicked Roman guard was watching the tomb in which Jesus of Nazareth had been laid. Knowing their very lives depended upon their vigilance, the eyes of the soldiers never dimmed, their bodies never relaxed as they carried out their assignment to keep any and all away from the tomb. No one was to get in. Certainly no one was to get out!

Suddenly, in the darkness, the ground began to rumble and shake as though a mighty rocket was being launched, and a violent earthquake erupted. Then, before the horror-filled gaze of the guards, against the inky blackness of night, an angel clothed in light as dazzling as new snow under a noonday sun descended from heaven, walked over to the tomb, rolled away the stone, and sat down on it! The guards passed out in terrified unconsciousness because they had seen past the angel and the rolled-away stone into the tomb! And the tomb was empty! JESUS OF NAZARETH HAD RISEN FROM THE DEAD! HE'S ALIVE!

God's Story

THE NARTHEX TO ETERNITY

"Now this is eternal life: that they may know you,
the only true God, and Jesus Christ, whom you have sent."

JOHN 17:3, NIV

Several years ago, I had the opportunity to visit Westminster Abbey in London. It is a grand cathedral where many of the kings and dignitaries of England are buried, and where the kings and queens receive their coronation. The narthex is small, dark, and cramped—just a brief space to pass through between the outside door and the door leading into the cathedral itself. I can't imagine anyone visiting the abbey and being satisfied to stay in the narthex. I also can't imagine anyone who would make an enormous effort to stay there with no thought to passing through to the glory of what lies beyond.

Your life and mine here on earth are like the narthex to a grand cathedral. Our lives are simply an area to pass through on our way to the glory of eternal life that lies beyond the door of death. Physical death for a believer is simply a transition into real life. And it's God's purpose that you and I live forever—with Him.

My Heart's Cry

ALWAYS NEAR

"I am with you always, even to the end of the age."
MATTHEW 28:20, NKJV

Following the resurrection of Jesus Christ but before His ascension, He spent forty days and nights, coming and going among His disciples. At one point, two of His disciples were walking along the road to Emmaus when suddenly Jesus appeared, walking with them. Then, just as suddenly, when they broke bread together, He disappeared. At another time that same day, His disciples were gathered together in the Upper Room in Jerusalem with the windows barred and the doors locked. Suddenly Jesus was in their midst; then just as suddenly He disappeared.

When Jesus suddenly appeared to His disciples then just as suddenly disappeared, could it be He was teaching His disciples to live by faith? Whether or not they could see Him, He seemed to be teaching them to be confident He was actively present and involved in their lives.

Even though you cannot see Him, you can know He is near because He says He is!

God's Story

ONE NEED

God is able to make all grace abound toward you,
that you . . . may have an abundance for every good work.

2 CORINTHIANS 9:8, NKJV

Twenty-five years ago, just about every self-respecting person in the South went to church on Sunday. But I knew the religious pablum the people were being fed didn't even come close to satisfying their emptiness within—because I knew *I* wasn't satisfied.

God used my need to make me aware of the needs of others. When a friend suggested that I do something about the spiritual starvation in our city, I actually laughed. But I started a Bible class that has multiplied ten times during the past twenty-eight years so that thousands of men and women have studied God's Word for themselves.

What need has God brought to your attention? Describe to Him what you see and how impossible it would be for you to do anything at all to meet that need. Then be alert to what He may reveal to you further.

Just Give Me Jesus

OCTOBER 5

THE MASTER DESIGNER

Your mercy is great above the heavens,
and Your truth reaches to the clouds.

PSALM 108:4, NKJV

When have you observed the blazing glory of
a tropical sunset

or the soft, silvery shimmer of moonlight on the
ocean waves,

or a baby's birth and first lusty cry,

or a bird weaving her nest, hatching and feeding
her young

and wondered, *who made it?*

When we thoughtfully consider the world
around us, we instinctively know our environment
is not some haphazard cosmic accident but the
handiwork of a Master Designer. The earth did not
come about by the snap of some giant fingers but
was deliberately planned and prepared in an orderly
progression of events. Like Planet Earth around us,
your life is not a haphazard cosmos, either. You were
deliberately planned to be filled with the beauty of
love and joy and peace and purpose—filled with
God Himself.

God's Story

THE MARRIAGE MAKER

He who finds a wife finds a good thing,
and obtains favor from the LORD.

PROVERBS 18:22, NKJV

My father once received a handsome Swiss watch from some good friends. After he had worn it for a while, the watch stopped working. When my mother took it to the local jewelry store, the repairman said he could not fix it. So Mother took it to another repairman and another. They all said it was beyond mending.

Not too long after that, my mother happened to be going to Switzerland, so she tucked the broken watch into her bag. When she arrived, she arranged for the watch to be sent to the company that had made it, explaining that it had broken and no one could fix it. Within a short period of time, she received the watch in the mail, running like new.

Marriage is God's idea. He "crafted" it. If your marriage is broken, all the "repairmen" or counselors you take it to will be unable to fix it. Take it to the Creator Who made it in the first place. He can make it work again.

Just Give Me Jesus

A PRIVILEGED POSITION

"You are my friends if you do what I command."

JOHN 15:14, NIV

What could be a greater privilege than to have Jesus call us His friend? If I told you that the president of the United States was my friend, you would probably snicker. And rightly so. Although I have briefly met him, I don't really know him, and any "friendship" is based on what I have read about him. But if the president of the United States stated that, "Anne Lotz is my friend," it would be impressive. It would indicate a relationship based on personal knowledge that he publicly affirmed.

Jesus did more than say you and I could call Him our friend. He promises He will call us *His friends!* Now that's impressive! That's a privileged position!

My Heart's Cry

"DO YOU LOVE ME?"

"Simon son of John, do you love me?"
JOHN 21:17, NIV

Jesus looked straight at Peter and asked for the third time, "Simon son of John, do you love me?" (John 21:17, NIV). Under the direct, searching gaze of his Lord, Peter must have known he was being asked whether he loved Jesus more than himself. This time did Peter squirm uncomfortably? Did he love Jesus more than the opinions of others, such as the servant girl in the courtyard? More than his own safety and comfort? More than his own reputation? More than his memories of sin and failure?

Jesus reached into Peter's heart and put His finger on Peter's motivation for service. Peter's motivation to live for Jesus and to serve Jesus was not to be an attempt to stave off guilt, or to earn forgiveness, or to avoid criticism, or to prove something to someone, or to gain approval or recognition. Peter's sole motivation in service was to be his love for Jesus, pure and simple.

Just Give Me Jesus

FOLLOW GOD'S DIRECTIONS

"Therefore, what God has joined together,
let man not separate."

MATTHEW 19:6, NIV

Don't break up what God the Creator has put together in an equal, diverse, unified companionship we call marriage. God is the God of the impossible. It does not matter how bad the condition of your marriage is. Turn it over to God, follow His directions, and He can mend the brokenness.

God has created everyone. Whether you are from Africa, America, or Asia; whether your skin is white or black or brown; whether you speak English or Polish or Spanish; whether your religious affiliation is Baptist or Buddhist or B'Hai; everyone is created by God. The entire human race comes with the Manufacturer's directions for a pattern to live by, a place to live in, a purpose to live for, and a partner to live with. Isn't it time you followed directions?

God's Story

THERE'S NO EXCUSE!

God is faithful, by whom you were called into
the fellowship of His Son, Jesus Christ our Lord.
1 CORINTHIANS 1:9, NKJV

"I have no one to help me into the pool when the water is stirred" (John 5:7, NIV). The man beside the pool of Bethesda was focused on what he lacked. He lacked a friend to help him. He lacked the strength to do it on his own. But while he was preoccupied with what he didn't have, he totally missed what he did have—*he had Jesus!* Standing right there!

What's your excuse for continuing to lie down on your responsibilities? What's your excuse for remaining a spiritual child when you should be mature in your faith? What's your excuse for sleeping when you should be kneeling in prayer? *What's your excuse?*

Is it lack of faith? Lack of willpower? Lack of knowledge? Lack of discipline? Lack of energy? There is no excuse you or I can come up with that is valid because we have Jesus!

Just Give Me Jesus

PAYING THE ULTIMATE PRICE

"No servant is greater than his master.
If they persecuted me, they will persecute you also."

JOHN 15:20, NIV

They didn't just persecute Jesus; they crucified Him! How is it that you and I think we will be treated any better?

You may be thinking this doesn't happen today. Yet it has been estimated by the *World Christian Encyclopedia* that more than 45 million men and women were put to death for their faith in Jesus Christ during the twentieth century! In recent years the estimate has averaged between 160,000 and 171,000 per year. Imagine! That's more than 10,000 Christians dying for their faith every month! More than 400 per day!

While you and I are getting up in the morning, trying to decide what to wear and what to eat and where we will spend our vacation, somewhere in the world someone is paying the ultimate price for his or her relationship with Jesus! And I ask myself, would I be willing to do the same?

My Heart's Cry

GIVE ALL THAT YOU HAVE

Philip answered [Jesus], "Eight months' wages would not buy enough bread for each one to have a bite!"

JOHN 6:7, NIV

Almost as soon as Philip came to the conclusion that it was humanly impossible to feed the crowd gathered on the hillside, "Andrew, Simon Peter's brother, spoke up, 'Here is a boy with five small barley loaves and two small fish, but how far will they go among so many?'" (John 6:8–9, NIV). While Andrew seemed to agree with Philip about the impossibility of feeding so many, his approach to the need was more positive. Without even realizing it, his faith had found the key to the storehouse of God's ample supply. When he offered Jesus a few loaves and fish, he was offering Jesus *everything* he had!

What do you have? Do you have a little bit of time? A little bit of love? A little bit of money? A little bit of faith? Don't concentrate on what you lack, concentrate on what you have. Then give *all of it* to Jesus for His use.

Just Give Me Jesus

GOD CARES!

God demonstrates his own love for us in this:
While we were still sinners, Christ died for us.

ROMANS 5:8, NIV

When have you felt so totally helpless that your prayer was fathoms deeper than mere words— it was a desperate heart's cry? Was it when some bad thing happened to someone you love? Was it when you experienced . . .

a physical illness?

a financial collapse?

a severed relationship?

a social rejection?

Did you think because something bad happened, it indicated Jesus doesn't really know what's going on? Or that maybe He knows, but He's not pleased with you? Or that *if* He does know, He just doesn't love you or your family enough to do anything about it? Are you interpreting His love *by your circumstances* instead of interpreting your circumstances *by His love?* When we are tempted to question whether or not God cares, we are reminded that, "God demonstrates his own love for us in this: While we were still sinners, Christ died for us." *God does care!*

Why?

OCTOBER 14

A SPIRITUAL IMPLANT

*"I tell you the truth, unless a man is born of water
and the Spirit, he cannot enter the kingdom of God."*

JOHN 3:5, NIV

The only people who go to heaven are
those who are born of water—those who have been
physically born. But those who go to heaven must
also be born of the Spirit. Just as the virgin Mary
conceived the physical life of the Son of God, you
and I conceive the spiritual life of the Son of God
when we are "born again." From that moment on,
we are essentially two people on the inside. We
have the mind, emotions, and will that we were
physically born with, but we now also have the
mind, emotions, and will of Christ within us. We
have a spiritual "implant" of the life of Jesus Christ
within our bodies. This is actually Jesus in the
person of the Holy Spirit.

This "implanting" of the life of Christ is a
supernatural miracle. It is something God does
in response to our humble confession and
sincere repentance of sin coupled with our
deliberate, personal faith in His Son. Have you
been born—again?

Just Give Me Jesus

OCTOBER 15

THE JEWEL OF CREATION

*"I have come that they may have life,
and that they may have it more abundantly."*

JOHN 10:10, NKJV

In the beginning, the Creator was not stingy with our environment. He filled it with life. Planet Earth was progressively transformed as every day God's Word went forth and every day God's Word was received. Each day's change prepared the environment for the next day's change until it was totally transformed. Yet it was as though it waited for something. In the same way a church sanctuary, all decorated, waits for the bride and a nursery, all equipped, waits for the baby, Planet Earth was prepared but waiting to be completed.

All of the daily changes seemed to be setting the stage for the climax on the sixth day. "Then God said, 'Let us make man in our image, in our likeness'" (Gen. 1:26, NIV).

Earth had been waiting for man! Man himself was the climactic jewel of Creation! *You* are His crown jewel!

God's Story

OUR FATHER COMES ALONGSIDE

If we live in the Spirit, let us also walk in the Spirit.

GALATIANS 5:25, NKJV

The Greek word for "comforter" is *parakletos,* which literally means one called alongside to help. This was beautifully illustrated in the 1996 Summer Olympics. As the runners in the 440-meter race flew around the track, one of them suddenly pulled up on the back stretch, and limped to a stop. He had pulled a hamstring! As the crowd stood, holding its collective breath, a man ran out of the stands to the young athlete. It was his father! As the television crew relayed the moving scene to the watching world, the microphones picked up the runner's words: "Dad, you've got to help me across the finish line. I've trained all my life for this race." And so the father put his arm around his son, and together, they limped across the finish line to a standing ovation!

In the race of life, our heavenly Father has come alongside us through the Holy Spirit. And when we think we can't go one more step He puts His everlasting arms around us, and gently walks with us to the finish.

Just Give Me Jesus

OCTOBER 17

NEVER ALONE AGAIN

In all their distress, he too was distressed; . . .
he lifted them up and carried them.

ISAIAH 63:9, NIV

The solution to loneliness is not to give in or give up. The solution is not to withdraw into an uninvolved, inactive life. The solution is found when you discover meaning in the midst of loneliness as God Himself shares your loneliness while you walk with Him and work for Him.

Two thousand years ago another solitary figure stood out in history. He stood alone against all the visible and invisible forces of evil in the universe. The sin of all mankind was placed upon Him as He walked to the place of sacrifice, carrying His own means of execution. He was betrayed by one of His best friends and denied by another. Not one person stood with Him—not the blind man to whom He had given sight, not the deaf man to whom He had given hearing, not the lame man to whom He had given strength. He was crucified on a Roman cross alone . . . so that you need never be alone—ever again.

God's Story

THERE IS NO PLACE GOD IS NOT

"I will never leave you nor forsake you."
HEBREWS 13:5, NKJV

Praise God that you and I can be where Jesus is—now, and for all eternity—because He lives within us and has promised that He will never leave us nor forsake us!

When your parents forsake you through death or abandonment, or your spouse forsakes you through divorce, you have His presence. (Ps. 27:10)

When the fire of adversity increases in intensity, you have His presence. (Dan. 9:1–25)

When you are overwhelmed by burdens or depression, you have His presence. (Isa. 43:2)

When you and I follow Jesus, He promises that we will be where He is. And there is not one place in the entire universe, visible or invisible, where He is not! What a blessing!

My Heart's Cry

FINDING LOVE

We love Him because He first loved us.

1 JOHN 4:19, NKJV

Our world is looking for love. As human beings, we need to love and be loved. But we're looking in all the wrong places. We look for it . . .

from a parent,

from a child,

from a spouse,

from a friend.

But our parents grow old and die,

our children grow up and live their own lives,

our spouses are too busy or too tired,

our friends are superficial or selfish.

Who can truly *understand* the need of the human heart? Who can *meet* the need of our hearts? *Where is love found?*

Love is found in the heart of God.

Just Give Me Jesus

OCTOBER 20

GOD REMEMBERS YOU

God remembered Noah and all . . . that were
with him in the ark, and he sent
a wind over the earth, and the waters receded.

GENESIS 8:1, NIV

When the text says God "remembered," it
simply means the time had come for God to act on
His own initiative, which required nothing of
Noah except patient waiting.

I wonder if Noah was just going about the chores
he had been doing every day for weeks and months,
feeding the animals, cleaning the stalls, when he was
startled by a shaft of light coming through the open
space just below the roofline. Did he drop his broom
and stumble over the feed bucket while scurrying
toward the upper deck and the window he had put
into the side of the ark? With trembling hands did he
throw back the shutters, gasping as the brilliant
sunshine stung his eyes? With his eyes watering and
his voice choked with emotion, did he embrace his
wife while he shouted his praise to the God Who had
sent the storm, but Who also sent the sunshine?
Noah knew God had remembered him! And God
remembers you!

God's Story

THE WONDERFUL SOMEONE

"If I go not away, the Comforter will not come unto you; but if I depart, I will send him unto you."
JOHN 16:7, KJV

The very promise Jesus gave us contains a name for the Holy Spirit that reveals the uniqueness of His nearness in our loneliness. This name, "Comforter," is equally translated from the Greek text into six other names, each of which describes a slightly different aspect of the Holy Spirit's ministry:

Comforter: One Who relieves of mental distress

Counselor: One Who gives advice and manages causes

Helper: One Who furnishes relief or support

Intercessor: One Who acts between parties to reconcile differences

Advocate: One Who pleads the cause of another.

Strengthener: One Who causes strength and endurance

Standby: One Who can be *always* relied upon

If you belong to Jesus, you have this wonderful Comforter working in your life. You have the Holy Spirit!

My Heart's Cry

WORK BRINGS SATISFACTION

If anyone will not work, neither shall he eat.

2 THESSALONIANS 3:10, NKJV

Are you afraid of hard work? Often we tend to quit a job before it is finished because the job is too hard or we lose interest or we receive a better offer somewhere else. The Creator has built into each of us the capacity for tremendous satisfaction in work that is not only finished but well done. If we quit before we are finished, we miss out on the satisfaction that comes with completion.

Sometimes we think of not having to work as a luxury reserved for the lifestyles of the rich and famous. It is actually a deprivation! One reason unemployment is so devastating is because when a person is out of work, that person is outside the Creator's design for living and therefore denied the satisfaction that comes from working and from completing a job.

What are you waiting for? Get to work and finish the job!

God's Story

FAITH THAT WORKS

"If you have faith as a mustard seed, you will say to this mountain, 'Move from here to there,' and it will move."

MATTHEW 17:20, NKJV

Are you discouraged because you have not received "anything from the Lord" as it relates to your prayer life? When Jesus' disciples were discouraged by their inability to get answers to prayer and so were ineffective in helping others, He encouraged them by pointing out that even faith the size of a mustard seed could move mountains. The key to faith that works is the foundation on which it is placed.

Base your faith in prayer on God's Word. Ask Him to give you a promise that applies specifically to your situation. Then claim it persistently in prayer until God keeps His Word.

Why?

PASSING THE BATON

"You shall know the truth,
and the truth shall make you free."

JOHN 8:32, NKJV

Winning a relay race depends not only on the speed of the runners but also on their skillful ability to transfer the baton.

In the race of life, the "baton" is the truth that leads to personal faith in God. Each generation receives the "baton" from the previous generation, runs the race to the best of its ability, then passes the "baton" smoothly and securely to the next generation.

Every day we see advances in our civilization bringing better health care, longer life spans, and ever-expanding knowledge. But underneath all the progress and sophistication, our civilization is experiencing a bankruptcy of moral and spiritual values that threatens to erode our very existence. In the midst of wickedness and waste, we must strive to relay the baton of truth that leads to personal faith in God that has been handed down to generation after generation since Creation.

God's Story

THE POTTER'S TOUCH

Does not the potter have power over the clay . . . ?

ROMANS 9:21, NKJV

Jesus makes suffering understandable; as the Potter, He uses suffering as the pressure on the wet "clay" of our lives. Under His gentle, loving touch, our lives are molded into a "shape" that pleases Him. But the shape that is so skillfully wrought is not enough. He not only desires our lives to be useful, but He also wants our character to be radiant. And so He places us in the furnace of affliction until our "colors" are revealed—colors that reflect the beauty of His own character.

But Jesus makes suffering understandable to this blob of clay. In the midst of the pressure and the heat, I am confident His hand is on my life, developing my faith until I display His glory, transforming me into a vessel of honor that pleases Him! I don't trust any other potter with my life.

Would you submit to the touch of the Potter's hand?

Just Give Me Jesus

OCTOBER 26

A SACRIFICIAL SACRIFICE

Do not forget to do good and to share,
for with such sacrifices God is well pleased.

HEBREWS 13:16, NKJV

Shortly before His crucifixion, Jesus was the honored guest at a feast held in one of His favorite homes. While Jesus, along with Lazarus and other guests, was reclining at the dinner table, Lazarus's sister, Mary, entered the room with an alabaster box. The box contained very expensive perfume—equal to a year's wages—that would have been her dowry. Mary took the box of perfume that represented her future hopes and dreams, broke it, and poured it on the head of Jesus. When she was criticized by those in the room as being exceedingly wasteful, Jesus sharply rebuked them while gently praising her for a beautiful act of sacrificial worship.

How extravagant is your sacrifice to God? Do you give God as little as you think you can get by with? A little bit of energy and effort when you're not too tired? A little bit of time you have no use for? A little bit of money you don't really need yourself? A sacrifice is not a sacrifice until it's a sacrifice!

God's Story

BELIEVE OR PERISH

"God did not send his Son into the world to condemn the world, but to save the world through him."

JOHN 3:17, NIV

Do you know someone who maintains that a loving God would never send anyone to hell? That a loving God will let everyone into heaven? Ask Noah! He was there when God shut the door of the ark. And although technically God doesn't send anyone to hell, you and I are condemned to go there if we refuse to enter through the "door" of the cross into the safety of the "ark," which is Christ.

God didn't want anyone to perish. He wanted all to repent of their sins and rebellion and enter into the safety of the ark. But the people refused.

The God Who saved Noah from His judgment by providing an ark is the same God Who so loved the world that He sent His only Son as an Ark—a hiding place from the storm of God's wrath. Whosoever believes in Jesus as God's gracious provision for salvation will not perish or come under God's judgment but will be saved and receive eternal life. *But you have to believe or you will perish.*

Just Give Me Jesus

SUFFERING IS NOT WASTED

Our light and momentary troubles are achieving
for us an eternal glory that far outweighs them all.

2 CORINTHIANS 4:17, NIV

Is the Potter molding—or remolding—you, using . . . pressure or problems? stress or suffering? hurt or heartache? illness or injustice? Has He now placed you in the fire so that circumstances are heating up with intensity in your life? Then would you just trust the Potter to know exactly what He is doing?

For the child of God, suffering is not wasted. It's not an end it in itself. Scripture reminds us, "For our light and momentary troubles are achieving for us an eternal glory that far outweighs them all."

The spiritual principle is that in some way God uses suffering to transform ordinary, dust-clay people into . . .

vessels that are strong in faith . . .

vessels that are fit for His use . . .

vessels that display His glory to the watching world.

So don't waste your sorrow. Trust God!

Why?

YOU ARE ON GOD'S MIND

I will not forget you.
See, I have inscribed you on the palms of My hands.
ISAIAH 49:15–16, NKJV

Noah was totally helpless to change his situation. There was nothing he could do except to stay on the ark and tend to the needs of his family and those of the animals until God in some way brought deliverance. He had to keep his faith in God while simply waiting out the silence that followed the storm.

Although He had been silent, God had not forgotten Noah. In fact, since Noah and his family were the only living persons on the face of the earth, we can be sure they had God's total, undivided attention every moment.

Do you think God's silence in your life means He has forgotten you? Oh, no! God says He has engraved your name on the palms of His hands. You are in God's heart and on His mind every moment. He is fully informed of your circumstances and will bring about change when He knows the time is right.

God's Story

FIXING WHAT'S WRONG

*By Him all things were created that are in heaven
and that are on earth, visible, and invisible.*

COLOSSIANS 1:16, NKJV

It can be mind boggling to contemplate the vastness of the universe, from the greatest star to the smallest particle. It is so vast that astronomers are now saying that it stretches beyond what we are capable of penetrating, even with sophisticated telescopes like the Hubble. And every bit of it was created by the Living Word of God, Who, even as He hung the stars in space, counted them and called them each by name!

Not only did He create objects of massive size, but He also created such minute, delicate, intricate things as snowflakes, no two of which are the same.

Jesus Christ is the One by Whom, for Whom, through Whom everything was made. Therefore, He knows what's wrong in your life and how to fix it. Let Him take charge. Give Him the authority to put it right.

Just Give Me Jesus

FAITH IN THE GOD OF CREATION!

*Sing praises on the harp to our God, who covers
the heavens with clouds, who prepares rain for the earth.*

PSALM 147:7–8, NKJV

Although God was actively involved throughout the Creation process, in the beginning the "earth was formless and empty." (Gen. 1:2, NIV) If you and I had been present to view the earth, we might have had the impression that God was not doing anything. Yet at that very time, "the Spirit of God was hovering over the waters" (Gen. 1:2, NIV). He was actively preparing Planet Earth to be transformed into a place of beauty and purpose.

Are you concerned for a friend whose life is like "the surface of the deep"—undulating, unstable? Even though you have prayed without ceasing, have you seen no evidence of God's activity in that person's life? Have you therefore concluded that God is *not* active? Place your faith in the God of Creation and be encouraged! He is *active* whether or not you and I can see evidence of His activity.

God's Story

Novenber

Jesus sees people as sheep
who need a Shepherd.

HOMECOMING DAY

"Rejoice because your names are written in heaven."

LUKE 10:20, NKJV

When I know that my loved ones are coming home, especially my son who is now married and living away from me, I begin to prepare for them. My son, Jonathan, loves barbecued spareribs on the grill, a homemade apple pie, and time to play tennis with his dad. I prepare those things for him, so that when he walks through the door of the house he will know he was expected and welcome, because this is his home!

Considering how I prepare for my children when I know they are coming home, I love to think of the preparations God is making for my homecoming one day. He knows the colors I love, the scenery I enjoy, the things that make me happy. All these personal details will let me know when I walk into My Father's House that I am expected and welcome because He has prepared it for me! And in the same way, He is preparing a glorious homecoming for *you*!

Heaven: My Father's House

A DIVINE APPOINTMENT

Truly my soul silently waits for God;
from Him comes my salvation.

PSALM 62:1, NKJV

Have you ever considered that you have a divine appointment when you get up early for your quiet time of prayer and meditation on His Word? That Jesus is patiently, personally waiting to meet with you there?

Have you ever thought of going to church as a divine appointment? That Jesus is patiently, personally waiting to meet with you there?

Have you ever thought of the Bible study you belong to as a divine appointment? That Jesus is patiently, personally waiting to meet with you there?

What a difference it would make in our attitude of expectancy and our habit of consistency if we truly wrapped our hearts around the knowledge that each *is* a divine appointment, that Jesus Himself is waiting to meet with us.

Just Give Me Jesus

DYING TO SELF

"If anyone would come after me, he must deny himself
and take up his cross and follow me."

MATTHEW 16:24, NIV

The power in your life and mine that results in blessing is in direct proportion to the extent that you are willing to die to . . .

> your own will,
> your own goals,
> your own dreams,
> your own rights.

It's what Jesus meant when He challenged His disciples, "If anyone would come after me, he must deny himself and take up his cross and follow me." However, before you get too hung up on the cross, don't forget—after the cross comes the resurrection and the power and the glory and the crown! Because Jesus was willing to die, He was blessed by God with a position of power and authority at His right hand.

If blessing is in direct proportion to a willingness to die to self, how blessed are you?   *My Heart's Cry*

NOVEMBER 4

GOD'S POWER TO CHANGE

His divine power has given to us all things
that pertain to life and godliness.

2 PETER 1:3, NKJV

Do you know someone who is desperate for change? Someone who is:

bound by anger?

isolated by pride?

depressed by worry?

consumed by jealousy?

panicked by fear?

God's Word has not lost its power since the beginning of time! The same power that transformed Planet Earth from that which was void, dark, without form, and in a fluid condition to that which was teeming with life is available today to change and fill empty lives. There is no life so shattered and devastated that it is beyond God's power to redeem and transform.

God's power changed the earth in the beginning, and His power is available to change you today!

God's Story

CUTTING AND CLIPPING

"Every branch that does bear fruit he trims clean
so that it will be even more fruitful."

JOHN 15:2, NIV

You and I can trust the Gardener to skillfully, personally, lovingly, and effectively prune the "vines" of our lives. Isaiah described the gentle skillfulness of His touch when he revealed, "A bruised reed he will not break, and a smoldering wick he will not snuff out" (Isa. 42:3, NIV). In other words, God will not cut you back so much that you are broken beyond the ability to grow, nor will He quench you to the point that you give up and quit. So trust Him. He's been pruning for years. He knows what He's doing.

While cutting is drastic and encourages new growth, clipping is used mainly to control and shape the growth of the plant. This encourages fruitfulness by concentrating the energy of the vine into the fruitful areas of the branch. So if you are being cut or clipped, stop complaining, start submitting, and look forward to the fruit.

My Heart's Cry

FORGIVENESS FOR ALL OUR SINS

If we confess our sins, he is faithful and just and will
forgive us our sins and purify us from all unrighteousness.
1 JOHN 1:9, NIV

The blood of Jesus is sufficient for the forgiveness of any and all sins because the cross was two thousand years ago and all of our sins were still to come. Therefore, all of our sins, whether we committed them yesterday or today or have yet to commit them tomorrow, are covered by His blood—past sins, present sins, future sins, big sins, small sins, or medium-size sins—it makes no difference.

Praise God for the blood of Jesus that is sufficient to cover all of our sins! *All of them!* Big sins like murdering your own mother. Little sins like gossip. Medium-size sins like losing your temper. They are all under the blood of Jesus, and we are free just to enjoy our forgiveness! We will never be held accountable for the guilt of our sins because Jesus has taken the punishment for us.

Would you thank Him now for your forgiveness?

Just Give Me Jesus

NOVEMBER 7

DROP YOUR ANCHOR

Work shall be done for six days,
but the seventh is the Sabbath of rest, holy to the LORD.
EXODUS 31:15, NKJV

God worked for six days during that first "week" then rested on the seventh: "And God blessed the seventh day and made it holy, because on it he rested from all the work of creating that he had done" (Gen. 2:3, NIV). The word *holy* means "set apart," or different from ordinary things.

From the law in Exodus we know one reason for this day of devotion is to ensure that we do not get too far away from God's pattern. If one out of every seven days we are anchored by our focus on Him, we are less likely to drift from Him. On the other hand, if one day each week is not spent in giving Him our attention, we are more likely to put Him further and further away from our thoughts until we do not seriously think of Him at all, and we end up being tossed about on the sea of life only to wind up being smashed and broken on the rocks when a storm hits.

Drop your anchor—keep your focus on Him!

God's Story

HEAVENLY TREASURE

"Store up for yourselves treasures in heaven,
where moth and rust do not destroy,
and where thieves do not break in and steal."

MATTHEW 6:20, NIV

We hoard gold, we wear gold, we invest in gold, we work hard for more gold—we love gold! We sacrifice our families, our friends, our reputations, our health—all so that we can increase our supply of earthly treasures. We want to buy more things . . .

so we can dust more things

so we can break more things

so we can get more things

so we can show off more things

—none of which will last!

Jesus commanded His disciples not to lay up treasures on earth where moth and rust corrupt and where thieves break in and steal, but to lay up treasures in Heaven. I wonder what treasures we will have in Heaven as evidence of our work and witness on earth—if any? While it is said we can take nothing with us to heaven—we can! We can take somebody else!

Heaven: My Father's House

THE WELL

*"Everyone who drinks this water will be thirsty again,
but whoever drinks the water I give him will never thirst."*

JOHN 4:13-14, NIV

Jesus knew the Samaritan woman who met Him at the well had searched for satisfaction and come up short. He knew her heart was empty, without love or self-worth or meaning or fulfillment or happiness. And so He gently pointed out to her, "Everyone who drinks this water will be thirsty again." What was "this water"? The woman took it to mean the water in Jacob's well, but Jesus was speaking to her heart. All those who look to draw their satisfaction from the wells of the world—pleasure, popularity, position, possessions, politics, power, prestige, finances, family, friends, fame, fortune, career, children, church, clubs, sports, sex, success, recognition, reputation, religion, education, entertainment, exercise, honors, health, hobbies—*will soon be thirsty again!*

If you look for deep, lasting satisfaction from any of these wells the world offers, you're wasting your time. Ask God now to fill you with the Living Water of Jesus Christ.

Just Give Me Jesus

A BRANCH THAT BEARS FRUIT

"Apart from me you can do nothing."

JOHN 15:5, NIV

Have you been making fruit-bearing more complicated and difficult than it is? Have you worn yourself out until you are discouraged over the lack of fruitfulness in your own service and resentful of others for the fruitfulness in theirs? Then I have wonderful news for you! You can relax! Not only are you freed from trying hard to bear fruit, you are freed from trying at all! That's the secret!

Fruit is produced on a branch that is attached to a vine. Jesus clearly told His disciples, "I am the vine; you are the branches" (John 15:5, NIV). So there is no guesswork about our position in His illustration. For a branch to have fruit-bearing potential, it must be alive. Since it has no life of its own, it must be organically attached to the vine so that the sap, or life, of the vine flows up through the trunk and into the branch. Fruit-bearing is all about being connected to the Vine. The branch bears the fruit, it doesn't produce the fruit. So . . . check your attachment to the Vine.

My Heart's Cry

WE CAN SEE GOD

No one has ever seen God, . . . God the One and only
[Son], who is at the Father's side, has made him known.
JOHN 1:18, NIV

All through the ages people have longed to actually see God. They have drawn pictures
and written books
and composed music
and constructed temples,
all for the purpose of unveiling the mystery of what He is like. But we are no longer left to our imaginations, wondering in educated ignorance. We can know for sure. Although "no one has ever seen God, . . . God the One and only [Son], who is at the Father's side, has made him known."

What a thrilling, firsthand, life-changing, mind-blowing, awe-inspiring testimony! God did not have to reveal Himself to us, but He did. He chose to make Himself visible in a way we could understand—as Man. This visibility is not only compelling and clear, it is glorious!

Just Give Me Jesus

WHERE ARE YOU?

*The man and his wife heard the sound
of the Lord God as he was walking in the garden in
the cool of the day, and they hid from the Lord God.*

GENESIS 3:8, NIV

I would imagine that up until this point, whenever God would come into the Garden Adam and Eve would run to meet Him like excited children. But when they harbored unconfessed sin in their hearts, His coming was a dreaded event. The thought of His presence was terrifying.

Adam and Eve were overlooking the single greatest truth in the universe! God loved them! He loved them in their sin so much that He sought them out! He did not leave them quivering in fear. He came.

God knew exactly where Adam and Eve were. He was not calling them to get information but confession. He wanted them to confront what they had done so they could set it right and be restored in fellowship with Himself. And where are you? Instead of hiding from God, would you run to Him? Confess your sin and enjoy reconciliation with Him.

God's Story

FATHER KNOWS BEST

The LORD is my shepherd; I shall not want.

PSALM 23:1, NKJV

Do you sometimes cry out, as I have, "God, don't You see my tears? Don't You see my broken heart? God, never mind me, but how can You bear to see the agony of my loved one? God, I know that You care. I just don't understand why You don't intervene in this situation right now. Why don't You do something? And, God, why did you do *that?!*"

Then, to my heart, I seem to hear His still, small voice whispering, "Anne, trust Me. I know what's best." And I'm left to wonder why I think I know better than God what's best for me or my loved one.

Why?

EVIDENCE THAT DEMANDS A VERDICT

Now the Lord is the Spirit,
and where the Spirit of the Lord is, there is freedom.

2 CORINTHIANS 3:17, NIV

And "where the Spirit of the Lord is, there is freedom" for you and me. Freedom from sin and selfishness and spiritual defeat and Satan's snares. Freedom to reflect Jesus as we are "transformed into his likeness with ever-increasing glory, which comes from the Lord, who is the Spirit" (2 Cor. 3:18, NIV).

As we live moment by moment under the Lordship—the control of the Spirit—His character, which is the character of Jesus, becomes evident to those around us. The outward evidence of His inward filling of our lives is His "love, joy, peace, patience, kindness, goodness, faithfulness, gentleness and self-control" (Gal. 5:22, NIV). Is there enough evidence of the Spirit in your life to demand a verdict from your closest friends and family members? The Holy Spirit empowers us, not just to *live* for Jesus, but to be *like* Jesus as He forms Christ within us. (Gal. 4:19)

Just Give Me Jesus

THE CORE OF A MISERABLE LIFE

Do not lose heart when he rebukes you,
because the Lord disciplines those he loves.

HEBREWS 12:5–6, NIV

The New Testament teaches us that we are not to "make light of the Lord's discipline, and do not lose heart when he rebukes you, because the Lord disciplines those he loves, and he punishes everyone he accepts as a son" (Heb. 12:5–6, NIV). God, as our loving Father, confronts us with our sin and convicts us of it in order to get us to confess. Because He knows if we do not confess and correct it, our misery will envelop us and we will live life at a very low level in comparison with the life He created us for.

If you and I resist confessing our sin when God brings it to our attention through our own Bible reading or through a spouse or a child or a friend or a pastor or just our own consciences, we harden our hearts. And a hardened heart is an impenetrable barrier in our relationship with God, in our enjoyment of His blessings, in our emotional and spiritual security, and in our eternal reward. A hardened heart is the core of a miserable life.

God's Story

A WORSHIPER GOD WANTS

God is spirit, and his worshipers
must worship in spirit and in truth.

JOHN 4:24, NIV

God wants us to worship Him in *spirit*. What does that mean? It means we must be indwelt by the Holy Spirit. We must be born again. It also means we must worship Him sincerely, earnestly, with a right spirit, with a sweet spirit. We are to worship from the depths of our beings as we are continually occupied with God.

God also wants us to worship Him in *truth*. What does that mean? It means there is no way to God, no way at all, without coming through Jesus Christ Who is *the* Truth. It also means that we must base our relationship with Him on His Word, which is the truth. And to worship Him in truth means to worship Him honestly, without hypocrisy, standing open and transparent before Him.

Are you the kind of worshiper God wants?

Just Give Me Jesus

OVERCOMERS

He who overcomes will inherit all this,
and I will be his God and he will be my son.
REVELATION 21:7, NIV

The apostle Peter confirms that the inheritance being laid up for the Father's children "can never perish, spoil or fade"—it is "kept in heaven for you" (1 Pet. 1:4, NIV). Although our inheritance is safely stored in heaven, there is a condition we have to meet before we can claim it: "He who overcomes will inherit all this."

What do you have to overcome in order to claim My Father's House as your own? You have to overcome . . .

your pride that refuses to acknowledge you are a sinner who needs a Savior.

your religiosity that substitutes . . . rituals for repentance, traditions for truth, and orthodoxy for obedience.

your unbelief that Jesus Christ is God's Son, the sinner's Savior.

Overcomers place their faith in Jesus alone for salvation . . . and inherit heaven!

Heaven: My Father's House

THE DOOR TO GOD

"I am the gate; whoever enters through me will be saved."
JOHN 10:9, NIV

The Shepherd's call has echoed down through the centuries. It's a clarion call to all sheep, offering freedom and salvation to those who are willing to come out of the . . .

> denominationalism,
>> traditionalism,
>>> ritualism,
>>>> agnosticism

of their religion and enter into a personal relationship with God. It's an authoritative command to turn away from sin and selfishness and walk through the open Door of salvation into the fold of a personal, permanent, love relationship with the Creator Who became our Savior.

Just as there was one door that led into God's presence in Eden and one door that led into the safety of the ark and one door that led into the inner sanctuary of the temple, a personal relationship with God is only accessed through one Door Who is Jesus Himself.

My Heart's Cry

NOVEMBER 19

HIS PLANS ARE PERFECT

My grace is sufficient for you,
for My strength is made perfect in weakness.
2 CORINTHIANS 12:9, NKJV

"Take with you seven of every kind of clean animal, . . . and two of every kind of unclean animal, . . . and also seven of every kind of bird" (Gen. 7:2–3, NIV). Just how big was Noah's assignment? We know that there are more than eighteen thousand species of mammals, birds, reptiles, and amphibians today. If the number is doubled to include two of every kind, with several thousand added to make up the additional pairs of each "clean" species, then double all of that to include any that have become extinct, the total is about seventy-five thousand animals!

According to the dimensions given, when Noah had all the animals assembled in the ark, only 60 percent of the available space would have been occupied. The remaining 40 percent would be available for food storage and living quarters for Noah's family. It all worked, as impossible as it had seemed!

God knows what He is doing! His plans are perfect!

God's Story

SO DRY AND THIRSTY

*"If you knew . . . who it is that asks you
for a drink, you would have asked him and he
would have given you living water."*

JOHN 4:10, NIV

While the woman of Samaria and I have many differences, we have one thing in common. I, too, find myself from time to time running on empty.

In the busyness of ministry,
    the weariness of activity,
        the excitement of opportunity,

I sometimes wake up and realize, "I am so dry and thirsty." Invariably, when I examine myself, the reason for the dryness of spirit can be traced to one thing. I'm not drinking freely of the Water of Life. I'm neglecting my Bible study. I'm rushing through my prayer time. I'm not listening to the voice of the Lord because I'm just too busy to be still. At those times I carve out quiet interludes to confess my sins and read and meditate and pray and listen and just drink Him in. Thank You, dear God, for still giving us today, Living Water from the Well that never goes dry.

Just Give Me Jesus

HIS TEARS ON MY FACE

The Lord God will wipe away tears from all faces.

ISAIAH 25:8, NKJV

God, as our heavenly Father, so closely identifies with His children that our tears are His. This precious revelation of God's relationship to us is first glimpsed plainly when we read how God called Abraham to leave Ur of the Chaldeans and follow Him in a life of faith, encouraging him by promising, "I will bless those who bless you, and whoever curses you I will curse" (Gen. 12:3, NIV). In other words, God would be so closely identified with Abraham that He would consider Abraham's friends and enemies His own. God not only loves His children, He identifies with them.

And in response to such loyalty and love, I, in turn, desire to so closely identify with Him—with His grief, His joy, His love, His pain, His blessings, His honor—that His tears are on my face.

My tears—and yours—are precious to Him! How He loves those who love Him enough to shed His tears as they share His cross!

My Heart's Cry

PERSISTENT PRAYER

"Ask and it will be given to you; seek and you will find;
knock and the door will be opened to you."

MATTHEW 7:7, NIV

When Jesus confronted a man beside the pool of Bethesda who had been paralyzed for thirty-eight years, He asked, "Do you want to get well?" (John 5:6, NIV)

At first, it must have sounded like a thoughtless question. Surely anyone who had been lying down for so long would want to get up. But Jesus knew it can be easier to lie on a cot letting people wait on you hand and foot, than to pick up all the responsibilities of life that are required when you can walk. The man answered that he did want to get well, and immediately Jesus told him to pick up his pallet, and walk. And the man did.

How do you and I show our eagerness to receive all that God has promised us? One way is through persistent prayer as we ask God for change, seek His Word about the change, then persistently pray until He brings it about.

God's Story

GRIEVING—BUT WITH HOPE

Brothers, we do not want you to be ignorant about those who fall asleep, or to grieve like the rest of men, who have no hope.

1 THESSALONIANS 4:13, NIV

When I was small, my grandmother lived right across the street from us. Whenever I got sick or just wanted someone to read to me or fix me something special to eat, I went across to her house. She read to me, played with me, fed me, and nursed me. When she died, I felt as if a part of myself had died.

Paul says it is all right to grieve, even twenty years after her death. But I am not to grieve as one who has no hope, because we believe that the same Jesus Who died on the cross to offer us forgiveness of sin, and the same Jesus Who was raised from the dead to give us eternal life is the same Jesus Who one day will come again! And when He comes, "God will bring with Jesus those who have fallen asleep in Him." When He comes, He will bring my grandmother with Him!

The Vision of His Glory

AROUND THE FATHER'S TABLE

Blessed are those who are invited
to the wedding supper of the lamb!
REVELATION 19:9, NIV

For the past several years, my husband and I, along with our family, have celebrated Thanksgiving at my father's house. . . . The meal is always abundant and delicious—turkey with dressing and gravy, ham, green beans, . . . my mouth waters just thinking about it! But the highlight of Thanksgiving is not the food, or the televised football games, or the fun. The highlight is always the fellowship around the dining room table. As we sip our coffee and gorge on one last piece of pie, my father presides at the head of the table as each person shares what he or she is most thankful for.

One day, in My Father's House, the table will be set and supper will be ready. One day all of the Father's children will be seated around that table. One day My Father's House will be filled with His family, and it won't get any better than that!

Heaven: My Father's House

SHAPED BY GOD

*The LORD God formed man from the dust of the
ground and breathed into his nostrils the breath of life,
and man became a living being.*

GENESIS 2:7, NIV

The Hebrew word for "formed" is *yatsar,*
which means "to mold." It is the same word used to
describe a potter molding and shaping clay. The
description reveals that while God *spoke*

> the worlds into space,
> the planets into orbit,
> the earth on its axis,
> the seas within their boundaries,
> the sun, moon, and stars to appear in the sky,
> the trees and flowers to cover the earth,
> the animals to fill the earth,

*God personally shaped the physical characteristics of
man with His own hands and breathed into man His
own life!* Such knowledge should cause us to pause
and worship the Creator Who molded you and me
from the "dust of the ground."

God's Story

FACING DEATH

God will wipe away every tear from their eyes;
there shall be no more death, nor sorrow, nor crying.

REVELATION 21:4, NKJV

In the beginning, death was not a part of God's original plan. He created you and me for Himself. He intended us to live with Him and enjoy Him forever in an uninterrupted, permanent, personal, love relationship. But sin came into our lives and broke the very relationship with God for which we were created.

When your loved one dies and your grief is tinged with anger, don't direct it toward God. He's angry too. Direct it toward sin and its devastating consequences. Dedicate yourself to sharing the gospel as often as you can. Pray that through your witness others who face physical death will choose to escape the second death, which is hell, the ultimate separation from God, by placing their faith in Jesus Christ. As we face death, our only hope is in knowing there is genuine, triumphant, permanent victory over it that is available to us in Jesus' Name!

Why?

GOD IN OUR MIDST

*"Whoever hears my word and
believes him who sent me has eternal life."*

JOHN 5:24, NIV

Every reject in the city must have gathered at the pool of Bethesda. The emaciated bodies and pain-deadened eyes gave silent witness to the helplessness of the diseased and disfigured who lay like discarded refuse at the water's edge. As the eyes of God scanned the mass of misery, He saw "a great number of disabled people . . . the blind, the lame, the paralyzed" (John 5:3, NIV). Each pitiful sufferer focused all attention on the water's surface, desperately pinning his or her hope on being the first to spot the bubbling movement and the first to react by jumping—or falling—into the pool. Each was totally preoccupied with his or her own disability.

The miserable were focused on the pool, on the water, on a traditional source of help—even as God Himself stood in their midst! Where is your focus?

Just Give Me Jesus

THERE IS STILL HOPE

*"Let all Israel be assured of this: God has made this
Jesus, whom you crucified, both Lord and Christ."*
ACTS 2:36, NIV

Pilate asked the mob a question that has reverberated through the centuries, "What shall I do, then, with Jesus who is called Christ?" They demanded with one voice, "Crucify him!"

Do you know someone who is rejecting Jesus today? Regardless of the vehemence of their words, or the hardness of their hearts there is still hope. Because some of the very men who had rejected Jesus on the Friday morning of His crucifixion later repented of their sins and received salvation! This astounding turnabout took place in the very place where Jesus had been condemned by the religious leaders when Peter preached a sermon at the Feast of Pentecost. Three thousand people repented of their sins and claimed Jesus as their Savior. So . . . don't worry about being rejected. Just pray and tell others about Jesus.

Just Give Me Jesus

NOVEMBER 29

CREATED FOR COMMITMENT

The LORD God took the man and put him in
the Garden of Eden to work it and take care of it.
GENESIS 2:15, NIV

Apart from understanding the work of God in our creation, there is no real meaning to human existence. If there was no Creator, then you are some cosmic accident, having come from nowhere and on your way to nowhere. You are just a nobody with no ultimate accountability or eternal value. Now that's depressing! Praise God, it's not true!

Where are you seeking lasting satisfaction? You may find temporary satisfaction in things and people, but permanent, deep, full satisfaction of your very being is only found in a right relationship with God for Whom you were created.

Not only is your *being* created for God, but your *doing* is created for God also. You and I were created for commitment to serve God. The Garden of Eden was not only a place for man to live, but it was a place for man to serve.

God's Story

YOU ARE ON GOD'S MIND

"I am the Alpha and the Omega," says the Lord God,
"who is, and who was, and who is to come, the Almighty."
REVELATION 1:8, NIV

This title describes the eternal omniscience of Jesus Christ. The alpha is the first letter and the omega is the last letter in the Greek alphabet. Through the alphabet all of our words, all of our wisdom, and all of our knowledge are expressed. Jesus is the beginning and end of the alphabet, the summation of all wisdom and knowledge.

What does the omniscience of Christ mean to me personally? It means I have always been on His mind. Think of it: The most important Man in the universe has always been thinking of you! Wonder of wonders! You have never been out of His thoughts! Even as He hung on the cross, He was thinking of you by name! Dying for you by name! And when He was raised from the dead on that first Easter Sunday, He was raised with you on His mind!

The Vision of His Glory

December

The testimony of one life
lived for Christ is powerful!

TIME ALONE WITH JESUS

Jesus often withdrew to lonely places and prayed.

LUKE 5:16, NIV

Often when I am under stress and pressure, I feel one of my greatest needs is to get a good night's sleep. But I've found that physical rest alone is not enough to revive my flagging spirit. I need the spiritual revival that comes from spending quiet time alone with Jesus in prayer and in thoughtful meditation on His Word.

A careful study of the life of Jesus reveals that as pressed as He was, He "often withdrew to lonely places and prayed." If Jesus felt He needed time alone in prayer with His Father, why do you and I think we can get by without it? How is your prayer life? Could some of the exhaustion you are feeling be the result of simple prayerlessness? How motivating it has been for me to view my early morning devotions as times of retreat alone with Jesus, Who desires that I "come with Him by myself to a quiet place" in order to pray, read His Word, listen for His voice, and be renewed in my spirit.

Just Give Me Jesus

WHEN THERE ARE NO ANSWERS

*These [trials] have come so that your faith . . . may result
in praise, glory and honor when Jesus Christ is revealed.*

1 PETER 1:7, NIV

What, or who, has . . .

turned on the tap of your tears,

and tossed you in your bed at night,

and preoccupied your waking thoughts,

and blackened your hopes for the future,

and broken your heart,

and wrenched an agonized "Why?" from your
trembling lips?

To our heart-wrenched cries of *Why?* God's
ultimate answer is, "Jesus," as He is glorified and
magnified in our lives through our suffering. Trust
Him. When guilt takes the edge off every joy . . .

when there are no answers to your questions . . .

trust Him when you don't understand.

trust His heart.

Why?

BECOMING MORE LIKE JESUS

*He who began a good work in you will
carry it on to completion until the day of Christ Jesus.*
PHILIPPIANS 1:6, NIV

The stronger I grow in faith, the closer I
draw to Jesus, the more I learn to love and trust
Him alone, the more disgusted, discouraged,
depressed, and defeated I become over sin and
failure in my life! I am sick of sin! *My sin!*

But there is hope for me! God's Word promises
"that he who began a good work in [me] will carry
it on to completion until the day of Christ Jesus."
What I will be like "has not yet been made known.
But [I] know that when he appears, [I] shall be like
him, for [I] shall see him as he is" (1 John 3:2, NIV).
Praise God!

One day I will no longer struggle with sin.

I will no longer stumble and fall.

I will no longer falter and fail.

I will no longer be tried and tempted.

One day I will be like Jesus!

The Vision of His Glory

ONE LIFE

If you confess with your mouth the Lord Jesus
and believe in your heart that God has raised Him
from the dead, you will be saved.

ROMANS 10:9, NKJV

Today, in a world where the role models are entertainers, athletes, and politicians, many of whom lack morals, integrity, and even common decency . . . in a world where no one seems to stand for anything unless it is to stand for selfish, self-serving rights . . . in a world where anything is compromised if it impedes success . . . in a world where there are no absolutes, where what is right is what works or what feels good . . . in a world where character no longer seems to count . . . In such a world, the testimony of *one life* lived for Christ is powerful! *One life* that confesses, "Jesus is Lord." *One life* that has the courage to stand for godly convictions in the midst of moral compromise. *One life* that tells the truth. *One life* that lives the truth. *One life* that lifts high the Light!

You can be that *one life!*

Just Give Me Jesus

THE LIGHT OF HEAVEN

"I am the light of the world. He who follows Me
shall not walk in darkness, but have the light of life."
JOHN 8:12, NKJV

Jesus said, "I am the light of the world," and He also said *we* are the light of the world. (Matt. 5:14) The sole light in Heaven will be the light that comes directly from God through Jesus Christ, and that light will be reflected in the life of each one of His children! The entire city will be saturated with the glorious light of His life, truth, righteousness, goodness, love, and peace—through you . . . and me!

Praise God! The Light of the World is the Light of Heaven! If all of God's children were like you, would Heaven be a "twilight zone"? What do you need to do today to clarify and intensify the reflection of His light in your life?

Heaven: My Father's House

RECEIVING HIS RESOURCES

Jesus went up on a mountainside
and sat down with his disciples.

JOHN 6:3, NIV

As Jesus and His disciples rested together on the mountainside, we have the beautiful picture of the Good Shepherd, making His sheep lie down in green pastures, leading them beside the still waters, that He might restore them on the inside. Jesus knew the demands that would be made on the disciples and Himself that very day, and He knew in order to meet those demands, they had to have some time alone together.

Again and again, I have been amazed to discover that the verse of Scripture or insight that God seems to give me in my early morning quiet time with Him is the very same verse or insight I am called on to give to someone else during the day. Jesus offers us ample resources, but we have to *receive* them from Him in order to impart them to others.

Just Give Me Jesus

START TRUSTING

"Do not let your hearts be troubled."

JOHN 14:1, NIV

"Do not let your hearts be troubled" is a *command* you and I are to obey! Deliberately calming ourselves is a choice we are to make in the face of

shocking setbacks,

catastrophic circumstances,

abrupt accidents,

irritating interruptions,

devastating dissension,

agonizing addiction,

frequent failures,

all of which cause us to be terrified of the consequences and repercussions. In the midst of the swirling, cloying fog of fear, Jesus commands, "Stop it!"

How in the world is it possible to obey a command that involves so much of our emotional feelings? Our obedience begins with a choice to stop being afraid, followed by a decision to start trusting God.

My Heart's Cry

DECEMBER 8

KING OF HEARTS

The kingdom of God is not eating and drinking,
but righteousness and peace and joy in the Holy Spirit.
ROMANS 14:17, NKJV

The Jews had many preconceived ideas
about the Messiah based on their interpretation of
Scripture and what they wanted. When Jesus of
Nazareth came on the scene with His public ministry,
He was neither the Messiah they had been
expecting, nor the Messiah they wanted. The Jews
wanted someone who would raise their standard of
living, and restore them to the world power they
had known under King David.

They wanted someone who would meet their
physical and material and emotional needs. They
expected a glorious, victorious king who would rid
them of the Romans and establish them in national
peace and prosperity and prominence. But the first
time He came, He came to establish the kingdom of
God, not in the world, but in the hearts of men. He
was born to die. And so He was rejected as the King
of Hearts. Then. But what about now? Would you
crown Him King of your heart today?

Just Give Me Jesus

DECEMBER 9

TURN ON THE LIGHT!

The unfolding of your words gives light;
it gives understanding to the simple.

PSALM 119:130, NIV

In the beginning there was no dawn to end the night,

> no sun to warm the day,
> no moonlight reflected in the swirling water,
> no horizon,
> just a never-ending night!

God didn't leave our environment in a murky, dusky twilight. "God . . . separated the light from the darkness. God called the light 'day,' and the darkness he called 'night'" (Gen. 1:4, NIV).

While the light described was literal, it has wonderful analogy and personal meaning for you and me, because *light* in the spiritual sense represents the truth, clarity, spiritual understanding, and discernment we receive from God's written Word. So . . . read your Bible and turn on the Light!

God's Story

ACCEPTED IN HEAVEN

God is not ashamed to be called their God,
for He has prepared a city for them.

HEBREWS 11:16, NKJV

After the long journey of life, we are going to look up and see heaven. We're going to see the glory of God radiating from within, and we're going to long for home. But we will be forbidden to enter. Heaven is closed to us because we are too dirty in our sin to enter it.

However, because Jesus found us in our hopeless, helpless state and offered us His hand at the cross, we can be welcomed into heaven. If we accept His offer and put our hand of faith in His, He will walk with us hand in hand, not only through the remainder of our journey, but through the gates of heaven that will be opened wide for us. We will be as welcomed and accepted in heaven as He is, solely because of our relationship and identification with Him. Praise God! Jesus is the One, and the *only One,* Who makes heaven available to the sinner, not only through the cross, but also through His resurrection.

Just Give Me Jesus

HE WILL BE LOOKING FOR YOU

"If I go and prepare a place for you,
I will come back and take you to be with me
that you also may be where I am."

JOHN 14:3, NIV

On the day when Jesus returns, everyone will be looking at Him. But have you ever considered where He will be looking? He will be looking for you! He has told us, ". . . I will come back and take you to be with me. . . ." His eyes will be searching the crowds of upturned faces, looking for you! While others mourn because His coming brings their judgment, you and I who have been redeemed by His blood will be rejoicing because His coming fulfills all our hopes and dreams!

Praise God for the deity of Jesus Christ! Praise God for the humanity of Jesus Christ! And praise God for the eternity of Jesus Christ!

The Vision of His Glory

THE CHOICES WE MAKE

I have chosen the way of truth;
Your judgments I have laid before me.

PSALM 119:30, NKJV

From the time we make the choice to open our eyes and get out of bed in the morning until we make the choice to go back to bed and close our eyes in the evening, our days are filled with a series of choices. We choose

where we go,

what we do,

what we believe,

and how we behave.

Our own lives, reputations, relationships, careers, health, future, and values are shaped by the choices we make. The choice

to lie or to tell the truth,

to seek vengeance or to forgive,

to ignore God or to acknowledge God,

determines the type of person we are. Without question, the most important choice you will ever make involves your attitude toward God and your relationship with Him.

God's Story

BLESSED ASSURANCE

Happy are the people whose God is the LORD!
PSALM 144:15, NKJV

Are you facing the future with eyes wide shut, teeth clenched, body tensed, dreading your tomorrows and what they may hold? Do you feel as though you are standing on the brink of a deep, dark abyss of helplessness and despair, caught up in events involving yourself or your loved ones that are beyond your control? Regardless of what those events may be, no matter your mental or emotional or spiritual state, God's vision of the future can fill you with hope right now.

You and I can look forward *WITH HOPE!* because we have the blessed assurance of Heaven, My Father's House!

Heaven: My Father's House

JESUS SAW PEOPLE AS GOD DOES

He had compassion on them,
because they were like sheep without a shepherd.

MARK 6:34, NIV

Jesus looked out at the approaching crowds and saw people who were seeking God but instead had received hundreds of manmade legal burdens.

He saw people who wanted truth but had received political posturing and religious platitudes from the Pharisees.

He saw people as more important than His own plans and need for rest.

He saw people not as an interruption, but as an opportunity to reveal His loving care and His Father's compassionate power to meet their deepest needs.

He saw people as sheep who needed a shepherd. He saw people *as God saw them.*

Just Give Me Jesus

BEARING MUCH ETERNAL FRUIT

*"You did not choose me, but I chose you to go
and bear fruit—fruit that will last."*

JOHN 15:16, NIV

Do you struggle with knowing the will of God for your life? Knowing God's will is not difficult—unless you are not abiding in Him. Jesus indicated that knowing His Father's will is the fruit of abiding as well as asking: "You did not choose me, but I chose you to go and bear fruit—fruit that will last. Then the Father will give you whatever you ask in my name" (15:16, NIV).

God has chosen you and me for the purpose of bearing much eternal fruit—fruit in our character such as love, joy, peace, patience, kindness, goodness, faithfulness, gentleness, and self-control exhibited toward those within our own home—fruit that is simply the character of God's Son coming out in us. We are to bear much eternal fruit in our service as we lead other people to faith in Jesus Christ and help them to grow into maturity so that they in turn will produce much eternal fruit in their lives.

My Heart's Cry

A PROMISE FROM GOD

He is my God, and I will praise him,
my father's God, and I will exalt him.
EXODUS 15:2, NIV

I have prayed without ceasing for my children throughout the years. One of the promises I believe God gave me for them, and a promise I have claimed again and again in prayer, is Exodus 15:1–2. This passage is the song of Moses as he exults in God's deliverance of the Hebrew children when the Red Sea was parted and they crossed over on dry ground. As Pharaoh's army pursued, the sea's walls collapsed, the enemy was supernaturally destroyed, and God's people rejoiced: *I will sing to the LORD, for he is highly exalted. The horse and its rider he has hurled into the sea. The LORD is my strength and my song; he has become my salvation.*

The promise God seemed to give me from this ancient hymn of joy was that He would supernaturally overthrow anything or anyone seeking to hinder my children from being in His place of blessing for their lives. God has a promise in His Word for your children, too. Ask Him to give it to you so that you can claim it in prayer.

Why?

UNCONDITIONAL SURRENDER

By this we know that He abides in us,
by the Spirit whom He has given us.
1 JOHN 3:24, NKJV

───────

When the Holy Spirit comes into you at your invitation, you receive as much of Him as you will ever have. You do not get a little bit of Him then and a little bit more at later experiences. Why is it, then, that He seems to get us in pieces? He comes to us unconditionally, while we surrender to Him conditionally.

We give Him our Sundays but not our Mondays.

We give Him our actions but not our attitudes.

We give Him our relationships but not our reputations.

We give Him our time but not our thoughts.

We give Him our burdens but not our bodies.

We give Him our prayers but not our pleasures.

We give Him our crises but not our children.

We give Him our health but not our hearts.

Would you drop the conditions and give Him all of you?

Just Give Me Jesus

CONFIDENT FAITH

Let the word of Christ dwell in you richly in all wisdom,
teaching and admonishing one another.

COLOSSIANS 3:16, NKJV

My parents were so confident in who God is and what God has said through His Word that it genuinely never crossed my mind to doubt God! When I was a child, I told my mother I wanted to know God personally for myself, and she lovingly gave me the instructions about how to approach Him. So I followed her instructions and went to the designated place at Calvary, to an altar of wood called the cross, and took my sacrificial Lamb. When I walked away from that altar, not only had I been reminded of my sinful condition, but I had the deep peace and assurance that my sins were forgiven! I was no longer separated from God but accepted by Him, because my sacrifice was the Lamb of God who is my Creator who became my Savior!

What a blessing to have parents who are people of confident faith. What a blessing to be a parent with confident faith like that!

God's Story

LOOK UP!

Blessed are those who do His commandments,
that they may have the right to the tree of life,
and may enter through the gates into the city.

REVELATION 22:14, NKJV

Has your entire life been a series of struggles?
Have you been . . .

More sick than well?

More defeated than successful?

More tired than rested?

More empty than satisfied?

More sad than happy?

Do you feel defeated because after a lifetime of
struggle, all you have to look forward to is death
and a cold grave? Look up!

Regardless of our circumstances or condition, we
can look forward *with hope* as we glimpse Heaven,
My Father's House, which is being prepared as an
eternal home for you and for me!

Heaven: My Father's House

EMBRACING GOD'S PURPOSE

*"I have brought you glory on earth by
completing the work you gave me to do."*

JOHN 17:4, NIV

Jill Briscoe, noted author and international
speaker, was recently asked what she saw as her life's
greatest mission. She answered that her life's greatest
mission is "to figure out what to do every day in my
life—as ordained by God—and then to do it." Jill
knows there are many things to do in life that are
not ordained of God, which is why we must be
single-minded.

To be single-minded as I embrace God's purpose
for my life means that there are times I have to just
say no . . .

to an invitation to join my friends for coffee,

to an offer for a lucrative job,

to a long weekend . . .

To be single-minded as I embrace God's
purpose for my life means there are times I have to
just say yes . . .

to less sleep and more prayer,

to less TV and more study,

to less work and more worship. *My Heart's Cry*

PLEASING GOD

The earth is the LORD's and all its fullness,
the world and those who dwell therein.

PSALM 24:1. NKJV

God is the Creator Whose purpose for you and me is the same as it was when He created our environment in the beginning. He wants us to reflect His image so that we might receive His blessing. "God saw all that he had made, and it was very good. And there was evening, and there was morning—the sixth day" (Gen. 1:31, NIV).

In the end, the Creator stood back. He surveyed the transformation of the environment that had followed His loving and careful preparation. Then He looked at the man and woman He had created in His own image, with a capacity to be His close, personal friends, and He was pleased.

As the Creator surveys your life, is He pleased?

God's Story

OVERSHADOWED BY THE SPIRIT

The Holy Spirit will come upon you,
and the power of the Most High will overshadow you.

LUKE 1:35, NIV

When the angel Gabriel appeared to Mary, he gave her the startling announcement that "the Holy Spirit will come upon you, and the power of the Most High will overshadow you. So the holy one to be born will be called the Son of God." When you and I place our faith in Jesus Christ and invite Him to come live within us, the Holy Spirit comes upon us, and the power of God overshadows us, and the life of Jesus is born within us. We do not conceive a physical life, but the spiritual life of Jesus in the Person of the Holy Spirit.

It is the indwelling powerful Person of the Holy Spirit Who sets me free from the habits of sin. But the power I possess to live a life pleasing to God is directly related to how much control of my life I give to the Holy Spirit.

Just Give Me Jesus

TRUST AND OBEY

Faith, by itself, if it is not accompanied by action, is dead.

JAMES 2:17, NIV

Jesus stands ready to help us, but His help is contingent on our absolute, total obedience to His Word, whether or not we agree with it or understand it.

In some way, God requires more than our intellectual faith—He requires our total trust as demonstrated by our obedience to His Word in order to release the miracle. Jesus gave sight to a man born blind, but in order to receive it he had to trust and obey by going to the pool of Siloam to wash. (John 9:1–7) Jesus gave strength to a paralyzed man who had been lying on his pallet for thirty-eight years, but he had to trust and obey by getting up and picking up his mat before he could walk. (John 5:1–9) Jesus healed a man with a withered hand, but before it could be straightened, the man had to trust and obey by stretching it out. (Luke 6:6–10)

What miracle are you waiting to receive? Could it be that God also is waiting—waiting for you to simply trust and obey?

Why?

GOD IS FULLY PRESENT

The LORD is near to all who call upon Him,
to all who call upon Him in truth.

PSALM 145:18, NKJV

On Christmas Eve, 1968, Frank Borman, James Lovell, and William Anders, while orbiting the moon in Apollo 8, were so aware of the Presence of God in space that they publicly read the first ten verses of Genesis to the listening world thousands of miles away. When James B. Irwin, an astronaut with Apollo 15, actually walked on the surface of the moon, he said he looked out into the inky blackness, saw our planet looking like a blue marble suspended in space, and was overwhelmed with the conscious awareness that God was present on the surface of the moon! And God was! And God is! He is not bound by space.

Whom are you praying for who is separated from you? A child? A spouse? What comforting encouragement to know that God is not only fully present with you but also with those from whom you are separated.

God's Story

HOPE WAS BORN

They shall obtain joy and gladness
and sorrow and sighing shall flee away.

ISAIAH 35:10, NKJV

The black, velvety sky was clear and studded with sparkling stars that had looked down on earth since the beginning of time. Shepherds appeared to be sitting idly by their flocks but in fact were keeping a sharp lookout for anything or anyone who might harm the sheep entrusted to their care. In the distance, the lights from the town could be seen and the noisy commotion could be heard as more people were coming into the town than the town could hold.

On the clear night air, sound traveled easily and somewhere from the direction of the village inn someone slammed a door.

And a baby cried.

The Seed of the woman, Who would open heaven's gate and welcome any and all who place their faith in Him . . . had been given!

The Hope that was born that night continues to radiate down through the years until it envelops your heart and mine.

God's Story

PHYSICAL AND SPIRITUAL NEEDS

Man is destined to die once,
and after that to face judgment.

HEBREWS 9:27, NIV

My grandfather was a medical missionary to China for twenty-five years. He established a three-hundred-bed hospital where his Chinese patients were cured of diseases and saved from death by his skilled ministrations. But in time, every single one of the people who went through his hospital died! If all my grandfather had accomplished was to meet the physical needs of these people, his efforts would have been hopelessly futile. But my grandfather was wise. He knew that "man is destined to die once, and after that to face judgment," and so all of his patients were given a Bible lesson and presented with the gospel of Jesus Christ. Hundreds, and even thousands, of Chinese men and women received Jesus Christ as their Savior at the Love-and-Mercy Hospital in Tsingkiangpu. And so many of my grandfather's patients who eventually died—still live. As you care for others, make sure you give priority to their spiritual needs.

Just Give Me Jesus

CREATED FOR GOD

Behold what manner of love the Father has bestowed
on us, that we should be called Children of God!

1 JOHN 3:1, NKJV

C. S. Lewis, in his testimony *Surprised by Joy,*
described his growing awareness of the capacity
within himself to respond with joy and delight in
such a way that it gave him an insatiable desire for
more joy and delight. The things he found so deeply
satisfying left him with a craving for more and more
satisfaction. He concluded that nothing in this
world could ever give him lasting satisfaction, so
therefore he must have been created for another
world. And C. S. Lewis was right. Our very *beings*
are created for God. We will never experience
permanent, personal satisfaction and fulfillment
apart from Him because, as Saint Augustine so
eloquently stated, "Our hearts are restless until we
find our rest in Thee."

God's Story

JESUS MEETS OUR NEEDS

"And I, if I am lifted up from the earth,
will draw all peoples to Myself."

JOHN 12:32, NKJV

Often, when I arrive in a city to participate in some conference or seminar, the organizers will take me aside and tell me privately about the people with broken hearts and broken hopes. And then they say, "Anne, we want you to know about so-and-so because we're hoping you will say something that will meet his or her needs." If I accepted that burden, I would be crushed under it! There's no way I can meet all those needs, so I usually respond with something like, "That's impossible! There are too many diverse needs. I can't address them all individually. But I can just give them Jesus." And again and again, I have seen Jesus personally meet the spiritual needs of the multitude—one by one.

Jesus has given me ample resources to meet the spiritual needs of others because He has given me Himself and He has given me His Word.

Just Give Me Jesus

JESUS CARES FOR YOU

Casting all your care upon Him, for He cares for you.

1 PETER 5:7, NKJV

Did you think Jesus only cares about things like heaven and hell? About forgiveness and sin? About holiness and wickedness? About truth and lies? About salvation and judgment? Jesus does care about those things. But He also cares about your job, about whether your child makes the sports team, about your children's college tuition, about your budget now that you are unexpectedly pregnant, about the roof that leaks, about the cranky transmission in the car, and about all the other physical problems and needs we face.

Jesus cares even if the physical problem we face is largely of our own making. He cares if we are having car trouble, even if it was caused by our not having taken the time to change the oil regularly. He cares if we are having financial struggles, even if they were caused by our having run up massive debts on our charge accounts for things we wanted but did not necessarily need. Jesus cares about your physical needs today.

Just Give Me Jesus

JUST THINK ON JESUS!

[He] loves us and has freed us from our sins by his blood.

REVELATION 1:5B, NIV

Jesus is the most important Man, not just in our nation, not just on planet earth, but in the entire universe! And He isn't important just for four years or eight years, but forever and ever and ever! Furthermore, the most important Man in the universe thinks I am so important, He gave His own life for me! How can I feel depressed by the smallness of my life when the most important Man in the universe died for me, rules over me now, and will one day return for me? In the eyes of the Lord Jesus Christ, I am important. I am of value. How can I consider myself anything less?

Do you feel depressed by the smallness of your life? There is an antidote for feelings of smallness. Just think on Jesus!

The Vision of His Glory

CHANGE IS POSSIBLE

Because Your lovingkindness is better than life,
my lips shall praise You.

PSALM 63:3, NKJV

No means of measure can define God's
limitless love . . .

No far-seeing telescope can bring into visibility
the coastline of His shoreless supply . . .

No barrier can hinder Him from pouring out
His blessings . . .

He forgives and He forgets.

He creates and He cleanses.

He restores and He rebuilds.

He heals and He helps.

He reconciles and He redeems.

He comforts and He carries.

He lifts and He loves.

He is the God of the second chance,

the fat chance,

the slim chance . . .

Just give me Jesus! He makes change possible!

Just Give Me Jesus

ACKNOWLEDGMENTS

Grateful acknowledgment is made to the following for permission to reprint material from the published works of Anne Graham Lotz:

The Vision of His Glory, (Nashville: W Publishing, 1996).

God's Story, (Nashville: W Publishing, 1997).

Just Give me Jesus, (Nashville: W Publishing, 2000).

Heaven: My Father's House, (Nashville: W Publishing, 2001).

My Heart's Cry, (Nashville: W Publishing, 2002).

Why? (Nashville: W Publishing, 2004).

NOTES

NOTES

NOTES